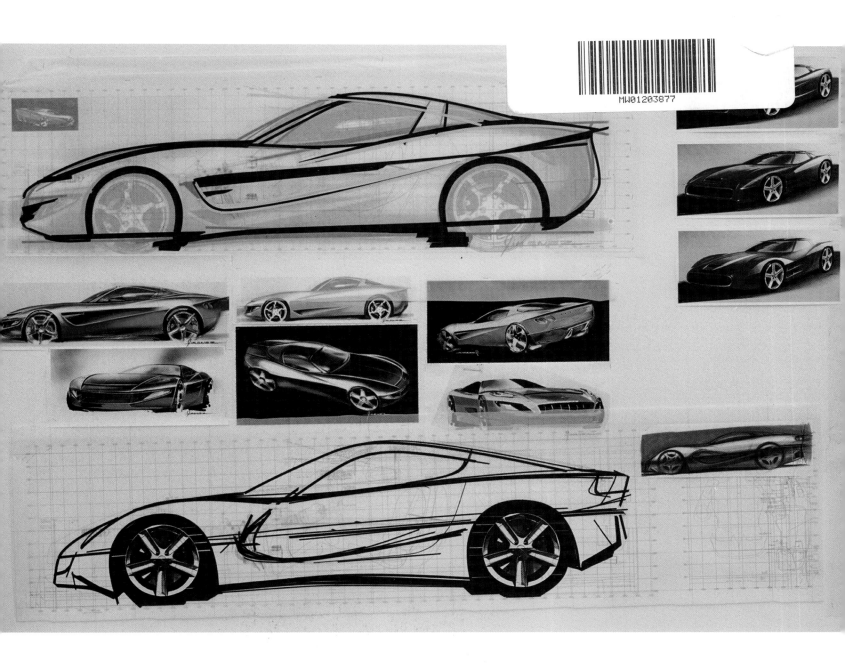

CORVETTE® C6®

PHIL BERG

MOTORBOOKS

First published in 2004 by Motorbooks, an imprint of MBI Publishing Company, Galtier Plaza, Suite 200, 380 Jackson Street, St. Paul, MN 55101-3885 USA

© Phil Berg, 2004

The information in this book is true and complete to the best of our knowledge. All recommendations are made without any guarantee on the part of the author or Publisher, who also disclaim any liability incurred in connection with the use of this data or specific details.

Motorbooks titles are also available at discounts in bulk quantity for industrial or sales-promotional use. For details write to Special Sales Manager at MBI Publishing Company, Galtier Plaza, Suite 200, 380 Jackson Street, St. Paul, MN 55101-3885 USA

ISBN 0-7603-1865-4

On the cover: Refinement—that's what engineers and designers at General Motors wanted most when they tackled redesigning the Corvette. Through their work, the sixth-generation of the car became shorter, sturdier, and sleeker.

On the frontispiece: The smaller back end of the revamped C6.

On the title page: The power behind the standard 2005 Corvette is a 400 horsepower engine, which is modeled after the powerplant of the 2002–2004 Z06 version of the car.

On the back cover: Two things of beauty: A sixth-generation Corvette and a moutain-filled landscape.

Edited by Leah Noel
Designed by LeAnn Kuhlmann

Printed in Hong Kong

Contents

Acknowledgments

I WISH TO THANK THE FOLLOWING FOR THEIR HELP IN
making this book become a reality:

- GM Communication's Dave Caldwell for his invaluable navigation skills around the GM colossus;
- GM Communications' Michelle Bunker in Bowling Green for her help getting photographs of the C6 taking shape;
- Renowned Corvette author Jerry Burton for his advice about the personalities and importance of the Corvette;
- *Automobile Magazine*'s Kirk Seaman for sharing his impartial views from his extensive interviews with Corvette team members;
- The entire Corvette team for letting me tag along;
- Joe Polimeni, Al Van Der Kaay, Tom Froling, Todd Fast, Tom Peters, and Richard Prince for their photography;
- And MBI Publishing Company's Leah Noel for reeling me back to English when I began to sound too much like an engineer.

Dreams Fulfilled Here

I COULDN'T HELP BUT SAY "MERCY!" when we first started discussing replacing the C5. Year after year, we had been pumping new technology into the C5 and always had stretched pretty far in making each year's C5 significantly better than the previous one. Plus, the C5 had stood the test of time, and we were proud of the breakthroughs we had achieved at its introduction and its subsequent upgradings, which were benchmarks for premium sports cars. So how would we improve a new Corvette to the extent the customer might expect on a whole new generation?

Because the C5 was unexpectedly successful, GM was ready to invest in a new Corvette so we could continue that streak. With that backing, we created the C6 as a true and worthy sixth generation—meaning truly everything that applies when you say "new Corvette." We've progressed from this very daunting assignment to something we're very proud of.

Dave Hill, Corvette executive and chief engineer, gets behind the wheel of a 2005 Corvette at Virginia International Raceway in spring 2004.

I vividly remember the day when I first saw a Corvette. I was in Little League, and someone drove a brand new Corvette next to the baseball diamond. It was 1953. Of course, our baseball game stopped. Everyone wanted to look at this car. I was 10 years old, and that Corvette left a powerful impression on me. So it's no surprise that since that day I've always been an observer and fan of Corvettes.

In 1970 the first new car I bought was a Corvette, while I was working as an engineer for GM's Cadillac division. Then, through a remarkable turn of events, I got the chance to join the Corvette team in 1992. I consider it a daunting responsibility, and it's one I take great satisfaction in performing.

Yet, I'm just a leader of a team that is filled with dedicated people; all of them have a lot of drive and determination to excel. That includes everyone, from the guys who scrape the clay models in the very beginning of the program to the assembler who puts the car together in Bowling Green. Everyone on the team feels a sense of importance in what they do. They know their work represents the best that America has ever achieved in the world of sports cars. It's easy for me to lead a group like this because we have such determined people on our team.

As I write this, the world still hasn't experienced how great the new Corvette is. Soon, the good news about the coupe and convertible will be out, but the new Z06 is a year away. The greatest part about it is that we were able to accomplish everything that we set out to do on the C6. Its total performance sets new standards in acceleration, top speed, racetrack performance, and braking for both the coupe and the convertible models. And while total performance is increased, so have the other values of the car. The interior has been enhanced, something really needed and successfully accomplished, and the car's entertainment, navigation, and satellite communication systems have all been upgraded.

The C6 stands out surprisingly from its predecessor by being substantially quieter, more refined, and perfected. You feel really good about the car because of that. But what the heck does quietness have to do with a sports car? Those of us who built this car feel this quietness adds value, makes the driving experience more enjoyable, and reduces fatigue on trips. So with it, the C6 becomes a fantastic touring car.

The C6 has many attributes and levels of excellence that I hope drivers will learn to appreciate and admire. I say this because the Corvette team is not in the transportation business. We're in the business of fulfilling dreams. So savor the freedom of the open road and enjoy the knowledge that you've got a car that can virtually overtake everything that's out there on the road or track. But also don't forget that the car does many things that you want it to do, but does them even better than you ever expected it could.

Dave Hill, vehicle line executive and
Corvette chief engineer

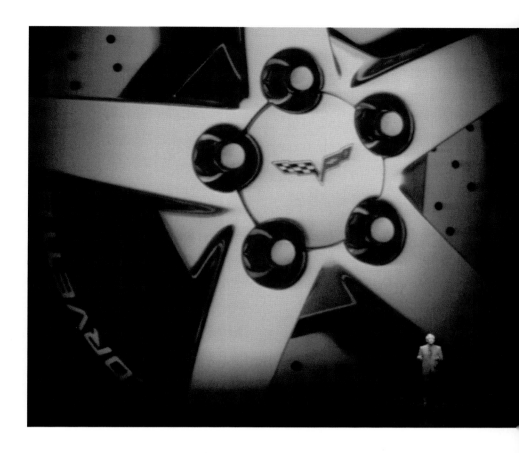

On January 4, 2004, after spending months tweaking its final design, chief engineer Dave Hill introduced the 2005 Corvette to GM employees and journalists at the Detroit Opera House.

Hill and members of the Corvette design team consider an early C6 concept at GM's design center.

Thanks to the success of the fifth-generation Corvette, Dave Hill and his team got a chance to rework the American icon for the twenty-first century.

One

Defining the New Corvette

Making America's Most Popular Sports Car Even Better

"Don't believe your eyes.
This car may look like the current Corvette
with fixed headlamps,
but it's an all-new interpretation of
the classic American sports car."

—Todd Lassa,
Motor Trend, February 2004

S IX GENERATIONS. FIFTY-TWO YEARS OF POWER, PASSION, AND PRECISION. American icon status. Despite all of these factors, the Corvette's long and storied history has been threatened more than once. When the car was just two years old, sales were a disaster and it seemed like the car was doomed. Even after the installation of the new small-block V-8 engine, the 'Vette didn't instantly become the beloved sports car that it is today. And from 1984 to 1996, during the production of car's fourth generation, the car was written off by many experts. They all agreed that this generation would be Corvette's last. The sports car market was floundering, and many automakers had stopped producing any new offerings.

Yet, the Corvette found a way to live on when the 1997 model, the fifth generation, was introduced. The fifth-generation Corvette's birth was delayed several years due to market conditions. However, thanks to quality and technological upgrades, it attracted more European buyers and had healthy sales in the United States. So, just two

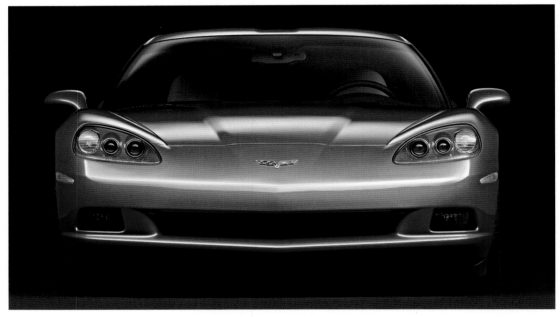

This page and opposite:

For the sixth generation, General Motors wanted a leaner and meaner Corvette, which translated into a car with a more taught competition profile and a more powerful engine.

years after the C5's introduction, those who had helped craft the latest Corvette saw room for even more improvements—changes that now could be fiscally warranted because the car had kept its solid customer base.

"The fifth-generation Corvette had all these little things that could not be fixed without a redesign. We wanted perfection in all these areas," says Dave Hill, who has been the chief engineer for the Corvette since 1992. "I would say we started passing notes back and forth in 1999. Then . . . we kept building the list, looking for more stuff, getting more customer input, thinking about things, thinking about fixes."

As he and other members of the Corvette development team dreamed about ways to make the C6 even better than the C5, the customer base for a new Corvette continued to grow and change. "The fifth-generation Corvette probably changed the face of the Corvette customer more drastically than any product

before it," says Rick Baldick, marketing director for the Corvette during the C5 era. "In the eight years [the] C5 was in existence, there was a sharp increase in average customer income and education, more college graduates, and the average household income went up considerably. [The resulting sales increase] was not because these customers needed it to buy the car, but because the car became such a terrific value. Even the Porsche owners who are dyed-in-the-wool, who will never have anything but a Porsche, will say, 'I've got to tell you—Corvette is a helluva value for the money.' I've never seen a car with more performance per dollar than you can get from the Corvette."

Yet while that value makes buying the Corvette more attractive, the car continues to be an "aspiration vehicle," Baldick says. "But [it's] an attainable aspiration. That's why sometimes the average age of our demographic has moved around a little bit. Some people will have to wait until a little later in life—get the kids through school, get

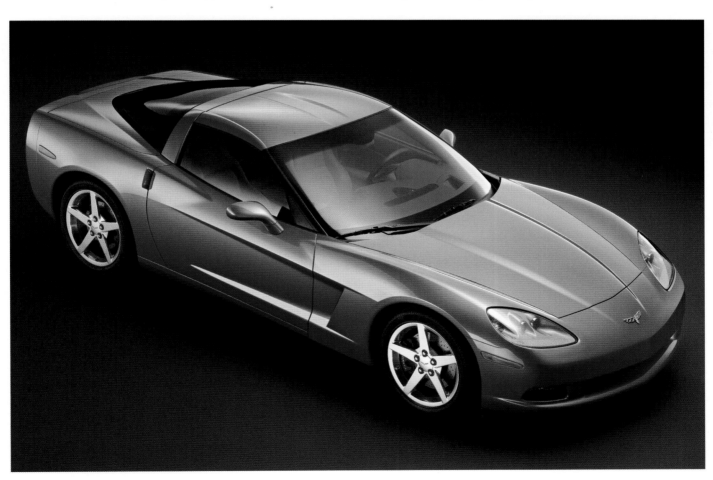

As part of making the Corvette leaner, engineers found a way to trim five inches from the car's length.

the house behind them, or whatever before they acquire a Corvette. It's a car they've always wanted. And just depending on how financially successful the person is in life, some get it at [age] 20; some don't get it until they're 46. But they've always known they're going to get a Corvette."

TARGETING PERFORMANCE AND POWER

Still, WHEN THINKING OF WAYS TO BROADEN that loyal customer base even further with the sixth-generation Corvette, General Motors executives knew that the new Corvette needed an even more refined, higher-quality reputation to silence the car's critics and overcome some of its persistent image challenges. "People sometimes say, 'That car looks good to me, but I hear it doesn't handle

very well,' or 'It squeaks and rattles.' These are perceptions that could be 25 years old," Baldick says. "That's what kind of drove us toward a more compact car. Tighter and quieter, the indexed glass, the reduction in road noise—where we want to be is truly a world-class car."

The result, Hill says, is a Corvette that is faithful to its history, but also pushes that legacy boldly forward. "This has been a car where, if everything is just working, you're not trying hard enough. So the new Corvette has gone from 90-percent perfect to 99-percent perfect. The sixth-generation Corvette is more solid, quicker, more confident, more refined, and more comfortable. You drive a C5 500 miles and still feel good; you drive a C6 600 miles and feel great."

Even though the C6 has a more European feel, it still looks like an American classic.

Lonely, twisty two-lane roads show off the sixth-generation Corvette's ability to handle tight corners.

Upgrades in handling and comfort were also made to the new Corvette so that it would be as purposeful on the road as it is on the track.

The C6 convertible is as equally purposeful-looking as a sports car as the coupe is.

Early Corvette testing at Grattan raceway involved team hot-shoes and Chevy racing drivers.

Driveline engineer Ian Bigsby and exhaust engineer Patrick Hoover check noise and temperature levels on a development car in the early morning hours at the desert proving grounds in Phoenix. When making decisions on how to rework the Corvette, the development team always thought about ways to reduce the noise level, which customers didn't like.

To achieve this, the Corvette team took GM Chairman Rick Wagoner's concept of "stretch" to heart. By stretching, designers and engineers decided to be more risky in calculating the technological progress they could make with the C6. They decided how they wanted the new Corvette to perform, despite the fact that they did not know how to solve the technical problems that would enable that performance.

"One thing we didn't have any idea how we would ever be able to do was make a huge difference in the road noise, because we tried to make the fifth-generation Corvette OK for road noise, but we just knew that for the sixth generation we had to get the road noise silenced by a very sizable amount. Every time we had a choice that could affect road noise, we took the direction of no noise. Tires, suspension hardware, bushings, powertrain values, and structure and acoustics inside the body—every one of those things had to be added together painstakingly to get road noise out of the car. That one was the one [where] we all said, 'We don't know how the heck we're going to do it; all we know is we've got to do it,' " Hill adds.

For the sixth-generation Corvette's performance target, the development team decided that the performance of the 405-horsepower Z06 version of the Corvette, built from 2002 to 2004, would be the standard for all 2005 Corvettes. But the Z06 wasn't the only target. "You know where the competition is now, and where you think the competition has the capability to be when the C6 comes out. You think about how much [of a] performance upgrade the customers are willing to pay for, or are expecting, and then you ask if we will be able to exceed these expectations," Hill says.

To get to this point, "we work on the whole car," he adds. "The shift knob is just as important to us as the sound of the exhaust; we tried to bring everything to a very high level of perfection. The fifth-generation Corvette gave us an unusual opportunity just to take something that was very good and make it almost perfect. And that's what we set out to do."

"Porsche and Ferrari are further out. They're ahead of us in power on some models, but they sell that stuff

for a huge amount of money and get poor fuel economy. We consider value an area where we're strong. In the C6, the brakes are heavier than in the C5, the friction contact on the road is bigger, the drivetrain is able to withstand more horsepower—those are the areas that we spent more in mass. But we saved mass in a lighter engine, a lighter exterior. And we've never had OnStar, XM satellite radio, or DVD navigation systems before; we've never had side air bags, so there are a lot of new features, but our value is still there."

On top of that, he adds, "I'm satisfied with the driving of the C6." That's important because Hill is the new Corvette's vehicle line executive (VLE), a General Motors' title that applies to the person who is responsible

Top: **Two racing drivers look over the engine during one of many 24-hour durability tests.** *Above:* **Test driver Mike Neal smiles about the new Corvette's performance during its 2003 development stages.**

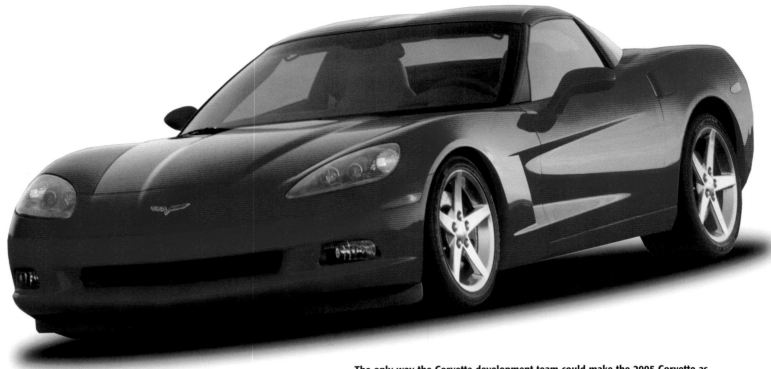

The only way the Corvette development team could make the 2005 Corvette as refined as it is, and meet its performance goals, was to use technology that was still being developed in the design process.

So what was the result of all the testing GM did on the recent C5 models and the C6 developement cars? The sixth-generation Corvette exudes the look of an exotic car and has abundant power, even though it remains an affordable option in the high-powered sports car market.

The Corvette convertibles have a hard speedster-style tonneau cover over the folded roof and "speedster" humps behind each headrest.

From the front, the silver convertible looks clean and ready to take on the open road.

The new Corvette's quarter-panel air opening is functional as well as aerodynamically slippery. Its vent treatment was inspired by wilder concepts on earlier models.

for every aspect of the car. As such, Hill is responsible for ensuring that the sixth-generation Corvette, with its 400-horsepower V-8 and 186-mile-an-hour top speed, lives up to GM's expectations. Those expectations include scoring well in performance tests, getting good marks for refinement, holding up well in surveys such as the J. D. Power suite of customer questionnaires, and still making money for the corporation.

Even more important to Hill is making sure the sixth-generation Corvette continues the car's legendary status. "With the Corvette, we're not in the transportation business," he says. "We're in the business of inspiring and fulfilling dreams."

ADDING A STYLING UPGRADE

To MEET ALL OF THOSE OBJECTIVES, THE SIXTH-GENERATION Corvette ended up being a blend of exorbitant power and speed, high-tech comfort features, and distinctive styling.

It's a delicate balance that's always been in play with this car. "It's about having the flair, the passion, but at the same time, it's like a jet fighter," Tom Peters, chief designer, explains. "It's all business. And this car is all business. It is a serious aesthetic, a functional aesthetic, because that's the environment this car operates in. You can have the 22-year-old guy or gal who's just cruising down to the club, but also you've got the guy who's going to be auto-crossing or racing at 150 to 175 miles per hour."

"Back in the Bill Mitchell days, the cars were designed to look cool, look fast, look aggressive, look sleek. For the performance [they'd say], 'Oh, don't worry about that. We'll put in a big block; we'll make that car perform any way we want to.' But in this day and age, we've got to design them to perform first and then figure out how to make them look neat."

So that was the challenge Peters faced as he started to draft the car's shape and structure.

The rear bumper of the car is trimmed as thin as possible to help reduce the length of the car, and the C6's license plate well is deliberately designed to hold plates from around the world.

Left: GM designers call the area between the seats of the Corvette the "waterfall."

The new grille pleased die-hard Corvette fans, who like the fact that the car now has a face again.

The C6 Team

Members who developed the Corvette's new interior pose with their final design.

Working on the Corvette is the equivalent of qualifying for the Special Forces unit of General Motors, an elite badge of honor for those who battle in the trenches of producing cars. The badge is deserved: Getting the sixth-generation Corvette built on time demanded a lot of dedication from the development team.

For one, just as engineers and designers thought that the new Corvette would be ready for a 50th anniversary launch, September 11th happened, leaving the economy in shambles. To sweeten lagging sales of new vehicles, most automakers started offering zero-percent financing deals. At GM, those deals hit the Corvette budget hard—the extra money to push the car's aggressive technology development was now gone.

The team had not planned for this setback, so when the budget finally allowed for resuming

development, engineers and designers had to resort to Plan B—working nights and weekends so that the car would be ready for customers by the fall of 2004. To add to the pressure, development schedules do not include any grace periods, or any extra time to allow for inevitable glitches.

In trying to make that production schedule work, Tadge Juechter, assistant chief engineer, decided to become a part of the wind tunnel testing team (even though it was not technically part of his job) while aerodynamicist Tom Froling never left the wind tunnel before 8 p.m. In all, about 200 engineers and 1,000 staff and operators at the Bowling Green assembly plant put in extra time to get the C6 ready for the 2005 model year. Outside of GM, suppliers contributed the car's tires, manual transmission, convertible roof, rear axles, interior module, body panels, and more specialized components so that the car would be ready to roll off the line in time and not go over budget.

During the process, both the suppliers and GM employees reported to the most senior members of the Corvette team: Juechter and Dave Hill, the Corvette's chief engineer and vehicle line executive. Below them, seven systems engineers managed the following divisions: interiors (Fernando Krambeck), electrical (Stan Modjeski), exteriors (Luke Ananian), structure (Ed Moss), HVAC and cooling (Mark Pickering), chassis (Dave Zimmerman), and powertrain (Bill Nichols).

Even though assigned to work on a specific area of the car, every team member wore many hats to get the job done, some not part of a formal description. "Within the Corvette team, we all tend to operate that way," Zimmerman says. "There are boundaries theoretically: This is my responsibility and this isn't. But to get the car done, we operate more along the lines of what's needed to get a fantastic car out there to the customer." For Richard Quinn, the thermodynamic engineer who is responsible for the car's cooling, that kind of dedication meant that he spent a lot of time in wind tunnel and on the track to compile all the 2005 Corvette's drag and temperature numbers. "He has to go wherever he has to go to give the car the best performance," says Mike Neal, ride and handling engineer.

Quinn also is one Corvette team member that has worked on the car since the beginning and will stay with the team until the first car is built. Other Corvette team members, including chief designer Tom Peters, were busy designing other projects such as the new Buick Velite during the final two years of development of the sixth-generation Corvette. Though some team members have moved on to other projects, they are physically nearby in GM's mammoth technical center in Michigan.

There is no tangible reward for working so feverishly, but sometimes the duty is fun. "Last November we used Alaska for cold weather

Members of the development team discuss an early concept of the car.

calibration," says Mike Petrucci, calibration engineer. "Some mornings were minus 20 degrees, and we worked from four in the morning until nine at night, for two week's duration. It was a lot of work. There were changes in the tires throughout the development process, and the engine had evolved through the previous summer and we needed to make changes. We had a Sunday where we couldn't work on site, and so we took the car and toured the Alaskan range. The car still had the camouflage on it. You wouldn't believe the looks we got because every other vehicle was a pickup truck. And we're driving this Corvette on street tires on the Alaskan range."

The Corvette development process continued up until the first examples were built, which began in the spring of 2004. Petrucci was "the last one in the pool," the car's other engineers say, because he programmed the computers in the car each time a part was changed. "When a part was made heavier or lighter, it changed the balance of the car, and Petrucci had to recalibrate the computers to match the change," Neal says.

Judging from the mood of most of the engineers at the conclusion of the development of the car, moments such as Petrucci's impromptu Alaska drive made all of this hard work—done to get the car just right—worthwhile.

With such an angled nose, even diehard Corvette fans might not notice that the sixth-generation Corvette is shorter than its predecessor. Despite its decreased length, the car is more aerodynamic too. Its coefficient of drag is almost 0.28.

Two

Styling and Structure

Reshaping a Modern Classic

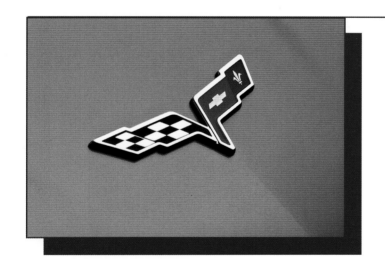

"It's a natural-born Corvette, which is no small feat, considering that the shape is fresh and familiar at the same time."

—Matt DeLorenzo,
Road & Track, February 2004

TOM PETERS TRULY HAD A TALL ORDER to fill when it came to finding a design that would suit the Corvette's passionate heritage, yet make the sixth-generation Corvette leaner, more compact, more taut, and more athletic so that it could meet its performance targets.

Through countless sketches, designs, and concepts, Peters finally found a shape that would stir 'Vette lovers' hearts and accommodate 186-mile-per-hour speeds. "The more you study it, the better you like it. It invites

inspection," Dave Hill, chief engineer, says. "The rear view is the most definitive, compared with the fifth-generation Corvette—Tom's been able to find ways to make the rear look compact, not overstated, with lighting that's really striking. In front the car now has eyes; its face is completed."

Peters doesn't remember the exact day he began drawing sketches of the new Corvette. He does know it was during the fall of 1999, just two years after the introduction of the fifth generation, that he started to draft

This C6 concept, from chief designer Tom Peters, was the one approved for the 2005 Corvette.

After the tough decision to make the headlights exposed, the design team had an easier task in agreeing on the new Corvette's grille opening, four taillights, and exhaust tips.

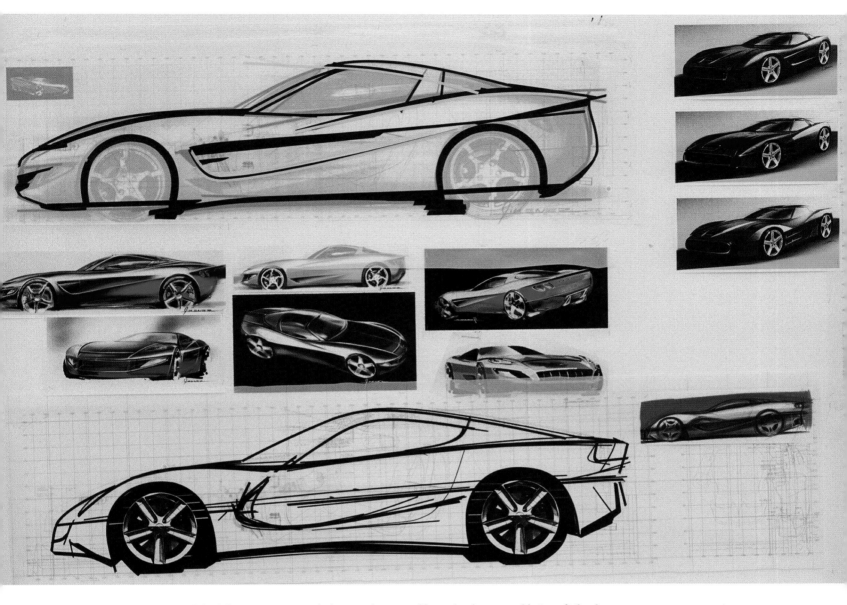

Before the full-size clay models of the new Corvette took shape, sculptors used large sketches as a guide to craft the clay.

many of the first concepts he had in mind. He was not alone in his efforts, though. Two other design studios became involved with producing Corvette concept sketches as well as models of their best ideas. One of those was GM's U.K. studio, led by designer Simon Cox, who also created the 2002 Cadillac Cien show car. The other was the independent Fioravanti studio, established by designer Leonardo Fiorvanti, in Turin, Italy. Fioravanti is well known for his work on some of Ferrari's most memorable models, including the 308 and the 512 Berlinetta Boxer.

The collaboration aimed to ensure that the design process invited fresh ideas. Also, Hill and Peters knew that it's not enough for the Corvette to be exclusively American. The true greats are respected all over the world. Outside of the United States, the American sports car is seen as being too ostentatious and lacking in quality and handling finesse—perceptions that most car enthusiasts agree are likely two decades out-of-date. But even without that image handicap, Corvettes are still considered too big for the narrow roads and parking spaces in European cities. "I drove a Porsche 911 and a C5

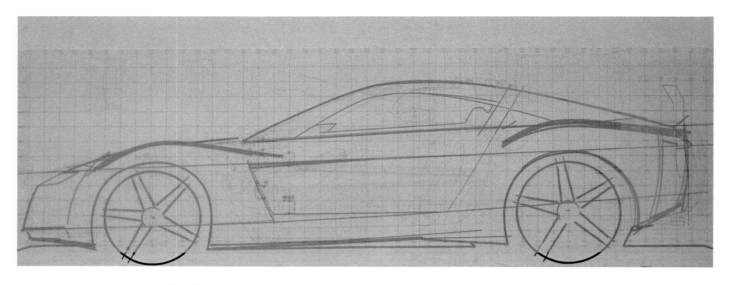

They also used a large taped outline to visualize the new Corvette's proportions.

These proportions were refined throughout the design process to give the C6 its final shape.

Corvette in Europe, and two things stuck out in my mind on those two experiences," Peters says. "One was [that] I like driving the Corvette there—it felt very comfortable on the autobahn and out on the more curvy roads. But driving the C5 in an urban environment wasn't as good. The 911 was perfect in an urban German environment. With the Corvette I felt very obvious; it felt too big."

Two of the models GM wanted to target most with the 2005 Corvette were the Porsche 911, priced at $65,000, and the Ferrari Modena, priced at $150,000. Despite the price disparity between these three cars, the Corvette needed to be leaner, meaner, and more contemporary to truly go head-to-head with the 911 and the Modena. "In the front, we wanted to make sure we did a center port opening. But you have different visions: Do you want staggered wheels and tires? Do you want round elements? Do you want strong side views?" says Peters, who came to GM in 1982 and worked on the design of GM's Chevrolet Camaro and Cadillac XLR before taking on the 2005 Corvette.

To help him make his initial ideas more concrete, he recruited fellow Corvette fans onto his design team. "It's not just one person. It's kind of a combination or synergy that makes it work," he explains. "I recruited guys like Kirk Bennion and Eric Clough as part of the key design team. Kirk has over the years had experience in designing Corvettes; he's a racing enthusiast, so he knows that aspect of the car inside out. [In] so many aspects, such as aerodynamics, Kirk might be one of the foremost guys in this company who really understand the automotive aerodynamics [of] high-performance vehicles. That's a key factor that affects the aesthetics of this vehicle. . . . Then Eric, to me, is the best interior designer in the organization. He designed all the interiors for the Cadillac XLR and the Cadillac Sixteen concept."

After all the players had a say on what they wanted to see in the new Corvette, team members compared their visions for the sixth-generation Corvette to the fifth-generation car. "The C5 is more of a nice, sleek, bubble shape," Peters says. "It's a very stylish car. We felt the next generation should push off that. The C6 is more

Designer Jeff Gale produced this model in 2000. It served as a guide through the whole styling development process and closely resembled the finished design of the car.

purposeful. We were talking about the car being a sign of the times, as well as following its lineage." It had to look like a Corvette, he adds, noting that the C6 also had to reflect the current age, yet not be considered "retro." "You always have the debate of evolutionary versus revolutionary, but it's hard to do a totally revolutionary car, especially with all the performance requirements that you put up against it."

The profile of the C6 was taped onto the side of a larger C5 to give the sculptors a clearer picture of the size of the new car.

Peters' biggest challenge came when the designers and engineers tried to find a shape that would hold up to top speeds. To reach that mark, the new Corvette needed to be more aerodynamic than any other previous design and the car's drag had to be very low. "We set the drag target collectively as a group. We wanted a 0.28 Cd (coefficient of drag)," says aerodynamicist Tom Froling. "That was the enabler to get to 180 miles per hour." By comparison, Mercedes' slick C-class sedan boasted the best aerodynamics for a production car when it was introduced with a reported 0.28 Cd, while a Dodge Viper measures about 0.40 Cd.

PROCESS OF ELIMINATION

To TRIM DOWN THE DOZENS of different concepts to favorite shapes early on in the process, top members of GM management reviewed the designs that would be made into small-scale clay models of the car. Of these models, slightly larger versions were made and then tested in the wind tunnel. "You get a handle on what the real proportion is, and then we start on the scale model. This is all leading up to the clinics," explains Peters, noting that clinics are the first presentation of the different versions of the car to the public. Of those concepts featured at clinics, Peters' team produced six designs, the U.K. studio presented four, and Fioravante delivered three.

"At this point, we're not going to pick a winner here," explains Peters, "We're doing an evaluation." But a couple of Peters' own designs fared well at the first clinics.

From the small-scale models that were selected as favorites, designers created full-size versions of the sixth-generation Corvette, including cars that were bisected

down the center with different designs on each side. These are called clown suits; they allow the designers and management executives to compare sizes and shapes. " We talk over what we did in the studio, and then the design is evaluated from a structure and engineering standpoint. The key in developing the design is getting it outside of the office and standing back and looking at it," Peters adds.

Finally, a design that is close to what can be built evolves, and a final clinic is held. For the 2005 Corvette,

Here, the three-dimensional model of the new Corvette continues to emerge from the sculptors' hands.

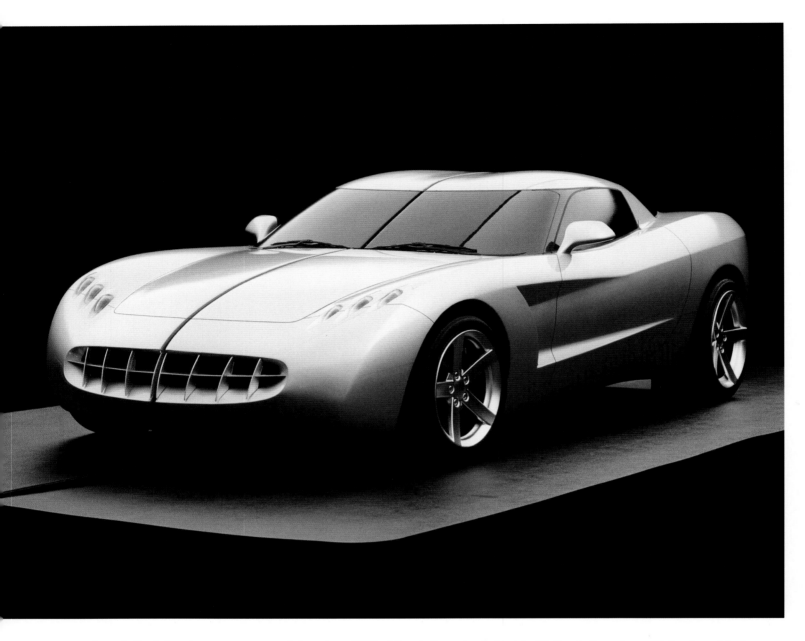

Above: **As the design schemes were narrowed down, two of GM's styling studios and an independent Italian studio made one-third-scale models of the new Corvette as its shape continued to be refined. GM designer Sang Yup Lee produced this model with retro cues to the SS Sebring Corvette concept.**

Opposite, top: **Chief designer Tom Peters created this model early in the design process. It features his favorite "double gills."**

Opposite, bottom: **General Motors' U.K. styling studio director Simon Cox contributed several models, including this one, to the development process.**

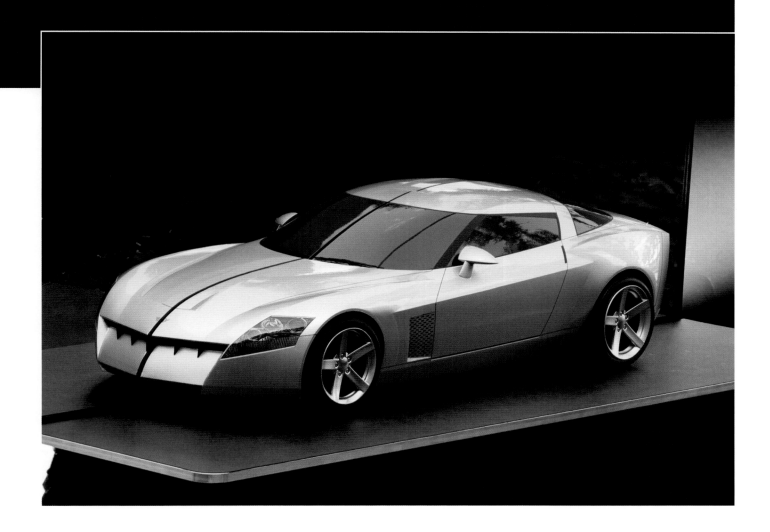

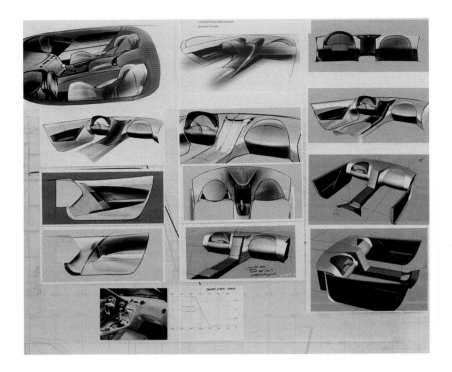

the final clinic happened in 2001 in Miami. "No other car conjures up such industry experts," Peters says. "It was unbelievable. We all have strong feelings, well, everybody has strong feelings about how a Corvette should look." However, the sixth-generation Corvette shown in Miami didn't look like the finished car. The design was "a little more edgy, or shear. It had more drive and more aim, and looked a little more dramatic [than the final car]," Peters adds. Following the Miami clinic, the design team spent several whirlwind months putting the finishing touches on the shape to bring its vision to life, as well as to make the car what GM executives and Corvette fans wanted.

"The DNA of Corvette is very powerful," Peters says. "But the reason I think it's sustained its popularity for such a long run is because it's colorful, simple, clean—not something that has had a wing and spoilers and other

Top and above: **The interior of the car was designed at the same time as the exterior, beginning with sketches such as these. Later it was modeled with clay onto a wooden form called a buck.**

Right: **The final product included both design and material changes, as the new Corvette's interior received a significant upgrade.**

This early full-size clay model shows that it was sculpted before the decision was made to expose the Corvette's headlights.

junk. It's just a classic form—round tail lamps, very simple five-spoke wheels, and simple front graphics."

He tried to keep those features in mind as he designed the C6, even when he was trimming the car's length and weight.

"If you look at the size, it's all part of the lineage, and it harkens back to the early 1960s," says exterior stylist Kirk Bennion. "It is part of its lineage for Corvette to be small and tight. Corvettes are very compact packages. We've got a lot in there. Wheels, suspensions, big tires, trunk—there's not a lot of wasted space there. But it's one of the most brilliant uses of space I've ever seen on an automobile."

In the end, Peters sees this difference in the size and attitude of the the fifth- and sixth-generation cars: "I think of the C5 as being like a hockey player, a big strong guy and he's in shape, but he looks like maybe he's had a couple of beers. The C6 is like Carl Lewis." It's lean and has a muscular body that has zero fat on it, he adds.

Yet to truly get the Corvette to an Olympic champion-sprinting ability, the C6 needed more tweaking than the flab that designers had already trimmed from the C5. The car needed more toning, almost 500 hours of it in the GM wind tunnel.

WIND TUNNEL TESTING

IN THE WIND TUNNEL, A NEW CAR'S trial-and-error testing takes on a whole new level. "There are some areas on

To get an early vision of the new Corvette's exposed headlights, the design team placed two surplus camera lenses into the fenders. These were initially held in by staples. The final headlight design relied on more compact lighting units, which were not available when the design process began.

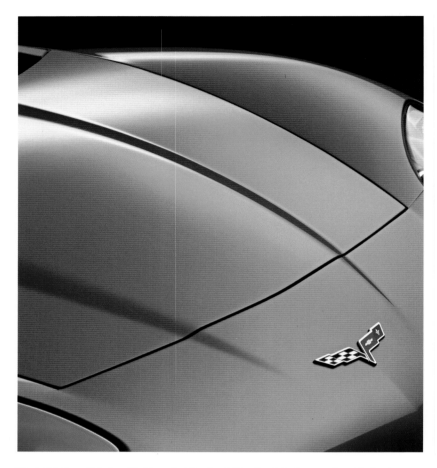

The 2005 Corvette's hood is hinged at the front, like the C5's; the new front badge is centered above the bumper.

that car you can change the surface around quite a bit. And then there are some areas where there are high-pressure areas and we can't touch it. You get it optimized. The front corners of that car required really, really long periods of development," aerodynamicist Tom Froling says.

Part of that challenge was redesigning the headlights. Designers and engineers spent about a year and a half on them and came up with 30 different versions before they found something that would work. In the end, the sixth-generation Corvette's headlamps became the most evident departure from the fifth-generation Corvette in the styling phase of the car's development. "The fact that the grille has exposed headlamps and the car's a front-breather—you haven't seen that kind of combination since '62," Froling says. "Exposed is the latest and greatest way to do things."

"Our big win was getting this to be a very tight, tight car," Bennion notes. Froling adds, "We wanted it to look neat, but at the same time we didn't want it to look neat and then say we hindered performance. So [we did] a lot of soul searching in the tunnel trying to find the low drag."

But Peters notes that no matter what you do, "exposed grilles will kill you in the wind tunnel." Other features also hindered the car's aerodynamics. First, the new Corvette's

For the final design, a single air opening in the front quarter panel won out over Tom Peters' original dual opening design.

The first public showing of a full-size concept for the sixth-generation Corvette was at a Miami research clinic, where this version of the car was displayed. But Corvette fans did not like the concept's sharp edges.

STARTING WITH A SOLID FRAME

BEFORE ANY DRAWINGS COULD SHOW what the new Corvette would look like, and before the shape of the car could be determined by designers, the car's foundation size had to be locked into the structural analysis computers at GM. That dimension was ultimately based on the size of the wheels and tires.

"You sort of have to know your wheelbase, what you want your dimensions of the vehicle to be as far as width and length, and then you've got to pick your tires and wheels very early on," says Dave Zimmerman, vehicle systems engineer for the chassis of the car. "Once you have that, then you can start designing all of the body and clearances that are necessary. So that starts defining where your inner wheelhouse is, where your outer wheelhouse is, [where] your inner and outer fender [will be]. Now you can start building your vehicle around that."

Stylists and aerodynamicists prefer longer shapes, which are easier to make sleek, but the car had to be shorter for maneuverability and handling. "It was all a lot of give and take all around," recalls structural engineer John Remy. "The design studio would tell us what they were trying to achieve, and we would tell them what we could make work, and we all worked together. We got what we think will be a high-quality car, very aesthetically pleasing, and it was from a lot of working together and a lot of hours. We really spent a lot of time trying to engineer the smallest sections, so that it's lighter. It's also much stiffer." Excess weight, the engineers stress, takes away from the rigidity of the car.

The biggest pieces of the C5 carried over to the C6 are its hydroformed steel rail perimeter frame and its integral center tunnel. But even these were modified significantly for the longer wheelbase and shorter overall length of the C6. To decrease the car's length, the frame rails were cut down by 2.4 inches. Then engineers added high-strength steel and braces to the frame to give the car more structural integrity. The additions also helped to reduce the chance of squeaks, rattles, and vibrations, while keeping the dynamics of the car feeling precise.

So after the clinic, the car returned to the styling studio for a makeover.

rear tires are wider than the C5's tires, making its frontal area larger and less aerodynamic. The C6 is also shorter than the C5, making it harder for air to detach as it passes the car and increasing the car's chances of creating drag-inducing turbulence. However, the wind tunnel aerodynamics weren't all working against the new car. The sixth-generation Corvette has slightly less ground clearance, and it is narrower; both factors aid its aerodynamics.

Yet Froling acknowledges the car's limits: "You're trying to do a car that needs a clean break of air at the back end and you can't get [it] as round or as more of a classic sports car kind of look."

Throughout this tedious wind tunnel testing, every small detail and square millimeter of surface was measured and shaped for least resistance. Bennion is pleased with the final outcome, and he is specifically happy with details such as the functional rear spoiler that is integrated with the center high-mounted stop lamp (CHMSL) and the rear diffuser that directs air past the four exhaust tips. He likes other details as well, including the rear license plate pocket that is designed to hold a variety of different-sized license plates from around the world.

Overall, the new Corvette's shape required a combination of sharp edges and complex radii, some of which could only be accomplished with the use of high-tech materials. The final shape is also smaller, but with a longer wheelbase tweaked to fit a redesigned chassis.

To further shorten the car, engineers changed the front bumper beam from a tube-formed beam to a beam made of two high-strength steel channels that are welded together. That alteration removed about two-thirds of an inch from the car's length; it also helped the designers and engineers reach a total reduction of 5.1 inches in the car's overall length. In turn, by cutting off 2.4 inches of the car's frame, engineers were able to slightly increase the Corvette's torsional stiffness.

Engineers also found a way to reduce the car's weight in the beams that make up the passenger cockpit. In the sixth-generation Corvette, these beams are made of extruded aluminum instead of the cast-aluminum parts that were used in the fifth-generation car. Cast parts have a slightly greater tendency to vary in size, while the more expensive extruded parts remain closer to their design size.

To further decrease the car's weight, more aluminum was used in the C6's body structure. Among those aluminum parts were braces that were added to the car's main frame rails to improve crash performance. The skid bar in front of the lower radiator in the new Corvette is also made of aluminum, and engineers cut 6.6 pounds from the car when they made the car's roof bow thinner. Engineers shed 4.5 more pounds with the car's side-impact aluminum beams, versus the steel of the C5. In addition, the doors don't have conventional latch and lock mechanisms inside, which makes them lighter and easier to close.

"We've come up with something where we're stiffer, we're lighter, we're less expensive, and we took a big metal beam out of what's in the back of the C5. So this is something we think ended up being a pretty solid win," Remy says.

Finally, another pound was dropped by using an aluminum panel in place of steel under the driveline tunnel of the car. This panel also has the advantage of adding stiffness to the structure.

The car's trunk and its instrument panel presented more opportunities for engineers to improve the car's rigidity. The trunk now has a lightweight plastic brace, and the instrument panel is held up by additional brackets, tying together the backbone of the car to the beam under the dashboard. This construction makes the car's steering feel more precise because the steering column is more firmly tied to the frame. The windshield frame also was made more rigid due to the extra gussets added at the A-pillars.

The science of how a car bends and wiggles is measured by Ed Moss, the systems engineer for the car's structure. "The philosophy of the sixth-generation Corvette is to enable a shorter, narrower car and continue to decrease mass. So the three things we're doing [are making it] smaller, lighter, but still stiffer. We still think this is a unique and effective way to do structure, especially for a convertible."

CHOOSING THE RIGHT MATERIALS

WHEN TACKLING THE TASK OF REVAMPING the new Corvette's composite body to fit the frame, the car's design and engineering team decided that it wanted to improve how the panels fit that frame. Team members also wanted to lower the weight of the panels, thus enabling better performance, and give stylists the

A C6 in profile with a C5, where it's easy to see how the Corvette's styling changed from one generation to the next.

Chief designer Tom Peters thinks the Corvette continues to be popular because its design is colorful, simple, and clean.

flexibility of making more complex shapes with high-tech materials.

After considering the weight versus strength of these materials, the team decided on five different types of plastic composites for the body panels. For the hood, doors, the trunk lid, and the top tonneau cover on the convertible, the panels are made of a polyester sheet molding compound (SMC) that is reinforced with fiberglass. This material can be molded into shapes like steel stampings, yet it will weigh far less than panels of the same size made of steel. The other advantage of the SMC material is that it doesn't rust like steel, and it will also hold up better in a hailstorm because it will resume its shape after small dings.

Corvette fans still refer to the car's body as fiberglass instead of composite, which is partially true. "SMC essentially is a fiberglass thermoset material," John Remy explains. The compound is referred to as such because it is made of fiberglass that is mixed with resin and compressed in a mold. "By compressing these, heat in the mold creates a chemical reaction," he adds. "Your panels cure and you essentially get fiberglass. On older

Corvettes, they either lay up fiberglass mats or spray fiberglass in molds and pour resin in. The SMC is a more efficient, more reliable technique."

The grille and rear fascia are made with polyurethane in a reinforced-reaction injection molding (RRIM) process, which allows complex shapes that could not be economically formed in steel or SMC. The front fenders are made of a special RRIM material that has the lightweight mineral micra added to reduce weight but retain the strength of normal RRIM. Complex tooling is required for producing the special RRIM parts, but the quality of the parts in shape, size, and strength is high. The RRIM parts cost more to make than the plastics used by most of the auto industry for fascias, but they hold up better to sunlight and dings.

The removable roof panel in the coupe is made of polycarbonate; it's either a thermoset type for the painted panel standard on the coupe or a transparent polycarbonate for the optional see-through panel. Both roof panels are made on the same tooling, although they do use different materials.

To fine-tune the car's shape so it could reach 186-mile-an-hour speeds, designers and engineers spent almost 500 hours testing it in the wind tunnel.

Above: **Aerodynamic work began on the Corvette's nose in 2000. Here, a clay front end was grafted onto a fifth-generation Corvette for testing.**

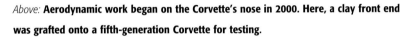

Above, right: **In May 2002, the Corvette team started using a full-sized clay model that closely resembled the car's final shapes in the wind tunnel. From here, designers only fine-tuned the car's curves and shapes to make it more aerodynamic.**

Below: **The team tried various rear fascia designs on a modified C5 so that engineers could find a way to reduce the Corvette's lift at high speeds.**

Small pieces such as the fuel filler door are made of GTX, a malleable plastic. This material is painted along with the rest of the body, and it also can be made to closer tolerances than other plastics. The 2005 Corvette is the first GM car to use this plastic.

By using the advanced RRIM material, engineers were able to noticeably cut weight in the body panels. The new car's hood is 15 percent smaller, but 35 percent lighter. It's also 40 percent stiffer, and it has a simpler hinge pivot that makes it easier to open and shut. Fourth- and fifth-generation Corvette owners are familiar with having to walk around the front of the car to press both rear corners of their cars' hoods to get them to latch. "The single-pivot hood really enables us to get effective closing efforts," Remy says. "You can't do that on a C5." A power pull-down latch on the rear hatch of the C6 coupe and fine-tuning the seals and hinges also contribute to making it easier to close.

The rear glass has a new pre-curved shape, but the area of the glass directly in the sight-line from the rear view mirror is flatter than it was in the fifth-generation Corvette. That eliminates the distortion that made a Ford Focus appear to be an Expedition in the C5's rearview mirror. By pre-curving the sides of the glass, "the glass panel gets deflected because of the loads from the seal and the gas struts," Remy explains. "You'll see loads on a hot day that are different from loads on a cold day. We used those loads; we didn't try to make the assumption that the hatch panel was infinitely rigid. So we predicted what those were with computers and tried to compensate by using the over-crowning technique of the glass to create something that would work in all conditions. So we're really happy with the way that turned out as well as how the cinching latch turned out. I think this hatch closes light-years better than the fifth-generation Corvette, similar to the way the hood does, and we're going to have a lot of happy customers because of that."

Customers are also going to be happy because all of these changes in the 2005 Corvette's shape and structure helped it to reach the top speed expected by its design team. Yet, finding an aerodynamic shape and sleek frame wasn't the only step to making the new Corvette faster than any other 'Vette—the development team also had to find just the right engine for the job.

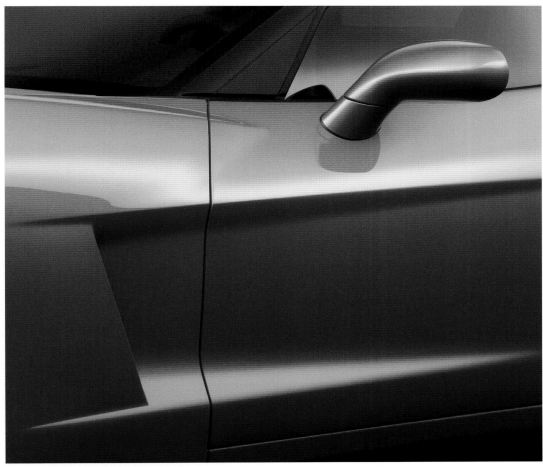

Although the side mirror looks the same as it did on the fifth-generation Corvette, it was subtly changed for the new car during hours of wind tunnel development. By making minute changes to the mirrors, designers and engineers reduced wind noise on the C6.

This cutaway model shows 2005 Corvette's console and floor composite panels.

Below: **Theoretically, the Corvette can be driven without the body, yet many of the composite panels improve the car's structure.**

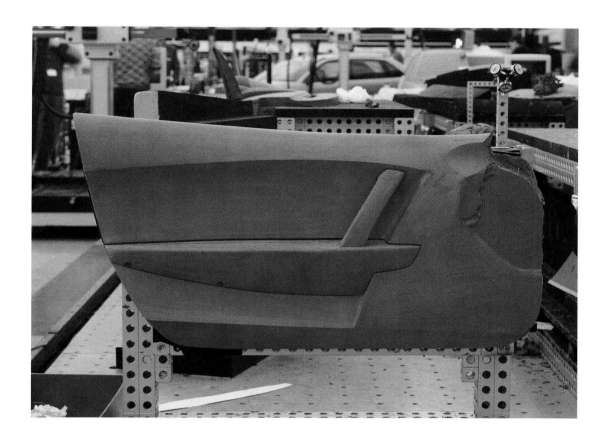

Here at left, the driver's door panel is shown as modeled clay, which was shaved and shaped for styling and function as its final design (shown below) takes shape. When the shape was chosen, designers and engineers used a polyester sheet molding compound (SMC) reinforced with fiberglass to make the panels lighter.

In the final design for the convertible, the Corvette design team used a tonneau cover to neatly hide the car's top.

Here, the tonneau cover opens as the top starts to come up.

Within seconds, the top reaches the windshield frame header and latches.

With its top up, the Corvette convertible still maintains the sharp shape of the coupe.

Because the Corvette's frame became shorter and lighter, it contributed to the car's increased strength. The roof bow on the coupe also is designed to add chassis stiffness when the hatch is attached. Theoretically, the Corvette can be driven without the body, yet many of the composite panels improve the car's stucture.

Overall, the new
Corvette's shape required
a combination of sharp
edges and complex radii.

The Ref

Integration is Essential to the Corvette's Personality

Exterior designer Kirk Bennion (left), who spent many hours working to integrate certain features into the C6's design, and engineer Rich Quinn prepare this development Corvette for another test.

Here's a call that needs a referee: "The shift knobs that actually feel best in your hand look hideous," Tadge Juechter says. "They're these blob-looking things, not pretty to look at at all. And the styling studio wants something that's beautiful to look at."

As assistant chief engineer, Juechter made the tough calls on such dilemmas during the development of the sixth-generation Corvette. And with the Corvette, GM's premier brand, engineers and designers push harder for their ideas than they would with more mundane cars. Plus, the balance of performance and style weighs more equally on the 'Vette than on other vehicles.

In the end, Juechter favored a shift knob is more functional than not, but still looks pretty darn good. "We made very small changes to the knob

toward that end, one millimeter here, two millimeters there," he says.

As Juechter worked on this multifaceted development process, he always kept one thing in mind—the car's "budget," not really a money matter but the finite limit of what can physically be added to the car for better performance, better looks, and better quality of assembly. "There's a budget for noise, budgets for fuel economy, and every other attribute," he says, adding that those budgets are eventually assigned dollar values for each piece and its desired behavior. "We have a dollar value for mass, a dollar value for electrical consumption.

"Everybody wants to throw something onto the car as if it has no cost to anything else, but it ends up affecting the rest of the car. If someone wants to add a feature to the car, but it draws an amp of electricity, eventually we end up upsizing the alternator and that adds weight to the front of the car."

That's not to say Juechter discouraged team members' ideas, though. In fact, Corvette engineers and designers were urged to stretch their imaginations. Then Juechter figured out what the costs of their suggested changes were in engineering terms. For example, while using bigger wheels and tires would help both the car's handling and styling, they would create more rolling resistance. "If somebody wants more rolling resistance, then we've got to get better drag or lower mass somewhere else. Special wheel styling might look cool, but it also might give you a lot of unsprung weight," he says.

One of the ways Juechter managed this balancing act was to get hands-on experience with the car. He and stylist Kirk Bennion worked together in the wind tunnel to strike one balance. "Kirk's got the aesthetics as his primary directive, but the shape has a huge affect on the aerodynamics, so he and I kind of balanced together how important the aesthetic is to getting

Left and next page:
Bennion, with the help of assistant chief engineer Tadge Juechter, spent many hours trying to find a compromise between what the engineering group wanted in a shifter and what the designers wanted. By making small changes, one millimeter at a time, they came up with a design that pleased both camps.

the aerodynamics we want," Juechter says. "We do this with trial and error—knowledgeable trial and error—in the tunnel. We do this on the clay cars, and say 'Couldn't we get this improvement by poofing this shape out here, pushing it in there, scrunching it in there, and maybe it won't drag as much?' So you find a way to maximize the studio flexibility with styling while still maintaining the aerodynamics we need."

The balancing act of integrating naturally conflicting components of the car begins early in the planning stages, which for the C6 started around 1999. "We started by balancing all of the requirements for the car. We wanted 400 horsepower, and we wanted fuel economy as good as it is with the C5. Then we asked what that means to all of the pieces that go into the car. Manufacturing is involved right from the beginning.

It's hard to think of a part of the car that is not influenced by manufacturing," Juechter adds.

Then while the car started to become more defined, Juechter led a formal meeting every Thursday morning called the "design integration activity." "We go through the car by geometric area–the rear compartment, the occupant compartment, and the engine compartment. We just slash the car into big pieces, and everybody who's got a part in that piece of the car is represented in the meeting. We talk about how the parts are going to go together–where the battery fits, what the hood blanket touches, and what happens when the engine rolls. We work out intricacies of wiring, HVAC lines, and front of dash pass-through. You can't put something sensitive to heat next to the exhaust like that."

Then if Juechter couldn't resolve a conflict, a program execution team–comprised of chief engineer Dave Hill and executives from finance and planning–takes it on. "We'd normally show them the car in the studio and say 'This is worth so many decibels of noise and so many counts of drag. What's everybody think? Are you willing to compromise someplace else to get this?' So the decision ends up being made as a team," Juechter says.

"This is a more refined version of the balance job we did with the C5. But since Dave Hill and I worked together on C5, we worked out the philosophy and the methodology already, and it's much more refined this time around."

When the development group decided to use larger wheels and tires on the new Corvette to boost its handling and styling, members knew they would be creating more rolling resistance.

The sixth-generation Corvette is powered by the fourth-generation of GM's legendary V-8 engine, which has always produced a lot of tire-smoking power.

Three

Pumped Up

Boosting the 'Vette's Power and Keeping It Driver-Friendly

"[The C6] had the same V-8 burble, fantastic throttle response, yet the shifter was better. Everything worked; it had more features; it was more comfortable. I thought if this costs the same as the old one, they'll sell every one of them."

—Larry Webster, top car tester for *Car and Driver* magazine

With the new engine, which produces 400 horsepower, the standard 2005 Corvette is capable of the highest top speed ever for a production Corvette coupe or convertible.

A T THE HEART OF EVERY CORVETTE is an engine capable of producing a surplus of tire-smoking power. When the small-block V-8 was first installed in the Corvette in 1955, this power became part of the Corvette's essence, an essence that hasn't faded despite the years and generations that the car has endured. So when the development team behind the newest Corvette started to redefine the car again, engineers and designers knew what the C6 needed—even more power. In addition, news of powerful new sports cars from Dodge, Ford, Ferrari, Porsche, and Lamborghini contributed to the team's desire to increase the Corvette's output.

Because of these factors, the standard 2005 Corvette is capable of the highest top speed ever for a production Corvette, even exceeding the performance of the exotic ZR-1 model (offered from 1990 to 1995). The new Corvette also has 400 horsepower, above the 2004's 350 mark, yet the 2005 Corvette will start under $50,000, which is an incredible value.

"The goal was set to achieve 400 horsepower, but to make the car acceptable for everyday driving with both the automatic and manual transmissions," says Bill Nichols, the vehicle systems engineer responsible for the powertrain. The engine also needed to meet guidelines for drivability and fuel economy.

ENGINE

FROM THESE GOALS, THE C6'S ENGINE was born. It is part
of a family of Chevy small-block V-8 engines, called Gen4
for fourth-generation. All four drivetrain combinations
available in the 2005 Corvette use this 400-horsepower
aluminum engine, and the standard configuration is a
four-speed automatic transmission. A six-speed manual
with closely spaced ratios is optional. An optional higher
rear-axle ratio is available with the automatic, and the Z51
performance package adds the optional higher rear-axle
ratio with the four-speed automatic or quicker gear ratios
with the six-speed manual, similar to the 2004 Z06. The
Z51 option is the fastest in acceleration.

The powertrain development team's first
consideration in revamping the small-block V-8 aluminum
engine that became the Gen4 was how to produce 400

Tucked neatly under the hood, the LS2 was purposely designed without turbocharging or supercharging.

horsepower without needing multiple valves and without the use of turbocharging or supercharging. "Simple was the best answer," Sam Winegarden says of the engine's concept. "Chief engineer Dave Hill said he would really like to take all standard Corvettes to where the Z06 was, and we said that jived with where we saw our competitors, from an engine perspective, going in terms of horsepower. We continuously benchmark our engines against our competitors and look at the trends."

Yet the team was concerned that engineers could design a naturally aspirated small-block to produce 400 horsepower without needing an expensive redesign. At that time, Corvette engineers considered using the existing 405-horsepower LS6 engine. "One might ask, 'Why not put the current 405-horsepower 5.7-liter in the

car?' That's do-able, but that has a lot of premium hardware in order to achieve more than 400 horsepower. The camshaft might be more aggressive than you want for an everyday car," says Nichols. There's also a flatter torque curve with the LS2.

When the group finished, the engine's peak output of 400 horsepower came at the 6,000-rpm mark, which is 300 rpm higher than the peak power point of the 2004 car's LS1. Peak torque comes at 4,400 rpm, where 400 lb-ft is produced, which is 25 lb-ft greater than the C5, 40 lb-ft greater with the automatic. The redline is now 6,500, up from 6,200.

Since Winegarden, chief engineer of the powertrain division's small-block development group, and his engineers had already been improving the small-block

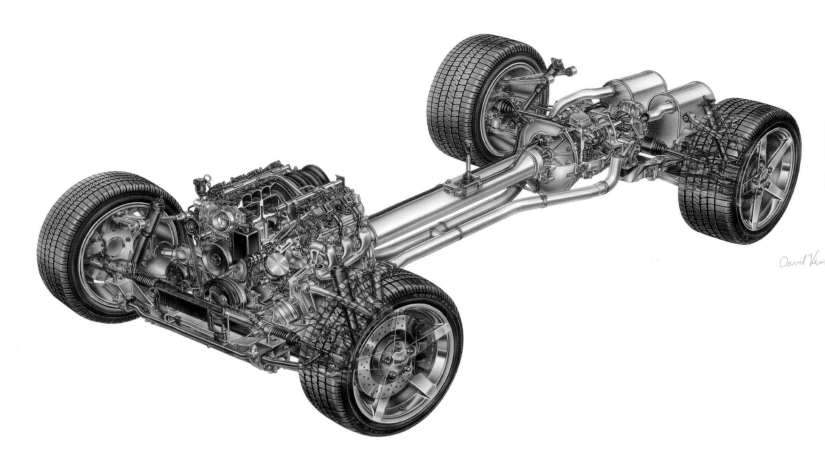

The new LS2 was moved about one inch forward in the frame of the new Corvette.

This new forward position allowed for a more efficient exhaust system, which in turn made the new Corvette more powerful. The increased power and torque is more than ample to exceed the traction of the rear tires.

This page and opposite:

While the new Corvette's power has been substantially increased over the fifth-generation car, its steering, handling, and braking abilities also have been bolstered.

V-8's efficiency and output to make GM's pickup trucks more fuel efficient, they had a leg up on making the LS2 engine in the Corvette meet these same standards. To see their vision for the engine become reality, the development group looked to increase the engine's compression ratio and to better squeeze the fuel mixture to extract the most energy. The downside was that by increasing the compression ratio the risk of premature ignition increased, but this risk was curbed with careful flow tuning and by adding sensitive electronic controls. "Our calibrations are such that you can drive the car with regular fuel. I appreciate the inherent efficiency with the fewest number of parts and perfecting the combustion to

attain the kind of performance you can out of the displacement," Nichols says.

Another emissions-friendly and efficient alteration came from improving the computers that communicate between the engine, transmission, and the electronic throttle. "We have a faster response to the input at the throttle and eliminate a component," Nichols says, adding that the electronic throttle control system helps emissions by damping unnecessary throttle movements that are occasionally made by fidgety drivers.

To increase output, displacement was enlarged from the 2004 LS1's 5.7 liters to 6.0 liters in the new LS2. In the preferred language of hot-rodders, that's an increase

from 346 cubic inches to 364 cubic inches. This displacement increase was accomplished by enlarging the cylinder bores from 99 millimeters to 101.6 millimeters, while the stroke has been kept at 92 millimeters. Despite the upgrades, the more powerful engine is no bigger on the outside than the Gen3 LS1. And even with its refinements, the block continues to use a precision sand-cast process and temperature-controlled cooling that

enhance the strength of the aluminum, and the iron liners are still cast in place. This was the same process successfully used in the third-generation small-block, the LS1.

The powertrain development team brought better breathing to the engine by using a higher-lift cam and by adding stronger valve springs from the 2004 LS6 to increase the engine's potential operating speed. The group

Hours of testing on the
famed Nürburgring
racetrack in Germany
refined the Corvette's
performance.

also patterned the engine's cylinder heads after those of the Z06 LS6 and optimized the combustion chamber for efficiency as well as power. The flow of the intake mixture and the shape of the LS2 combustion chamber allow an efficient 10.9:1 compression ratio, up from the 10.1:1 compression ratio of the LS1. Flat-top pistons further enhance the combustion process. "One of the things we found in this combustion chamber is the way the mixture is moved or swirled. It lets us actually bump up the compression ratio because the burn is more efficient," Winegarden explains.

A new engine control computer checks for the vibrations caused by detonation many times each second, and official word from GM is that premium fuel is recommended for maximum power, but not required. A

new floating wrist pin configuration is used to withstand the greater forces in the engine, and friction is reduced by using lower-tension piston rings.

The LS2 also benefits from a less-restrictive exhaust, which translates into more power. Developments in the rare metals that make up the insides of the exhaust catalysts improved their performance, resulting in less exhaust restriction. The more restrictive quad-catalyst design of the LS1—which used small secondary converters mounted close to the exhaust manifold—was not necessary to meet emission requirements with the LS2. Other subtle adjustments also enhance exhaust performance, including increasing the muffler's volume and routing the exhaust pipes carefully, so they have more gradual bends—which help eliminate noise during

The C6 is a combination front- and bottom-breather, which means that the engine intake and cooling air comes from both the grille and under the car.

When the Corvette team finished designing the engine for the sixth-generation Corvette, its peak output of 400 horsepower came at the 6,000-rpm mark, which is 300 rpm higher than the peak power point of the 2004 car's LS1.

accelerating periods between 1,500 and 2,400 rpm. Along with the single-catalyst-per-bank converter system, backpressure is reduced to help power output. For reduced cold-start emissions, the new catalytic converters have been mounted closer to the engine.

To boost the amount of space behind the exhaust manifolds for these catalytic converters, engineers and designers moved the engine forward in the new Corvette frame about an inch. This arrangement also provides the least amount of flow restriction. A revised oil pan with improved baffles allowed elimination of the "gull-wing" oil pan of the LS1 and LS6 engines and created additional

clearance for the exhaust. "The gull-wings take up real estate we'd like for other things, like the close-coupled catalytic converters," Nichols notes. This lighter pan, coupled with a windage tray and revised oil pickup, provides improved oil control during maximum cornering forces exceeding 1.0 g. Nichols explains that a 1.0-g corner will slosh the oil in the pan to its side, the same as tilting the engine 45 degrees. "We have a test stand that lays the engine right over at a 45-degree angle."

The crankcase ventilation is similar to that on the LS6, with an efficient oil/air separator located in the block valley. This design helps reduce oil consumed through the

PCV system during high-g, high-RPM cornering maneuvers. A lighter water pump with the same flow capacity reduces mass in the front of the engine.

An increase in the throttle body bore from 75 millimeters to 90 millimeters allows even more air into the engine's larger cylinders to make more power. Since the C6 is both a "front-breather," where air intake enters the engine compartment from the grill, and a "bottom-breather," with air coming from underneath the car, more air is available for the engine to burn. With all the Corvette's improvements, GM is particularly proud of the car's efficiency. It reaches 23 miles per gallon on the EPA combined city/highway test and is capable of producing 400 peak horsepower. This score is the highest in the world for a car with such a powerful engine. The 320-horsepower Porsche 911 scores only 20 miles per gallon on the same test, while the similarly powerful Ferrari Modena makes 400 peak horsepower and scores just 12 miles per gallon on the test.

Just as the Corvette team had hoped, turbocharging and supercharging were not necessary to achieve the output power needed for the sixth-generation car. "Now, when you want something that gets up to 600 or 700 horsepower, you're asking me to solve a different problem," Winegarden says.

SMOOTHER SIX-SPEED SHIFTING

FOR THE CAR'S STANDARD MANUAL TRANSMISSION, the sixth-generation Corvette uses a highly refined version of the fifth-generation's Tremec six-speed transmission. The new Tremec T56 has two sets of gear ratios, STD and Z51. The Z51 ratios are higher for maximum acceleration and are the same as those in the C5 Z06, except fifth gear is taller than on the C5 Z06 so that higher top speeds can be reached.

Overall, the improved transmission has lighter shifting and feels more direct due to the addition of new linkages and a shorter shift lever. "You want to feel fewer

A transmission cooler next to the radiator is used for both automatic and Z51 manual transmissions.

Durability testing for the sixth-generation Corvette involved it being driven over hundreds of hours and thousands of miles on regular roads as well as test tracks.

events going on as you're shifting, so it's a smoother shift," transmission engineer Bill Zabritski says. The shift lever has been shortened 14.5 millimeters, and fore/aft shifter travel has been shortened one inch. Inside the gearbox, the synchronizer travels were shortened by 10 percent. The lateral and longitudinal detents in the linkage have been modified to reduce efforts, and bearings have been added to the shift rails to lower friction. Internally stepped clutch teeth on the synchronizer sleeves engage sequentially and result in quicker synchronizer engagement, as well as a more precise feel. Although versions of the gearbox are also found in competing performance cars such as the Dodge Viper, the Corvette shift enhancement package is proprietary to GM.

Proprietary is usually a term that means "expensive" and limits development. Except in this case, the cost of developing the Tremec T56 will be spread to more than just the Corvette. "A lot of these improvements are going into other vehicles at GM, but Corvette's going to be the first usage of the stepped-teeth synchronizers," Zabritski says.

Other changes proprietary to the Corvette include an external fluid pump driven by the transmission countershaft that pumps transmission fluid to a cooler in the radiator. After being pumped to the cooler, the fluid in export models returns to a small, seven-plate heat exchanger attached to the left side cover of the differential and then to the transmission. This detour takes about 10 degrees of heat out of the differential fluid that is also pumped through the heat exchanger and is necessary because the car needs to be able to run at top speed on a full tank of fuel without overheating any component.

Even with the improvements, the team grudgingly accepts one device on the transmission that helps fuel economy, not driving pleasure. Known as computer-aided gear selection (CAGS), it improves fuel economy numbers, using a solenoid to force the driver to move the shift lever from first to fourth gear, skipping second and third. CAGS was first added to the Corvette in 1989, although its range of operation takes place only when the throttle is opened 20 percent or less and when the car's

Increasing the displacement and the compression ratio for the LS2 V-8 resulted in the biggest power gains over the LS1 V-8, which was used in the fifth-generation Corvette.

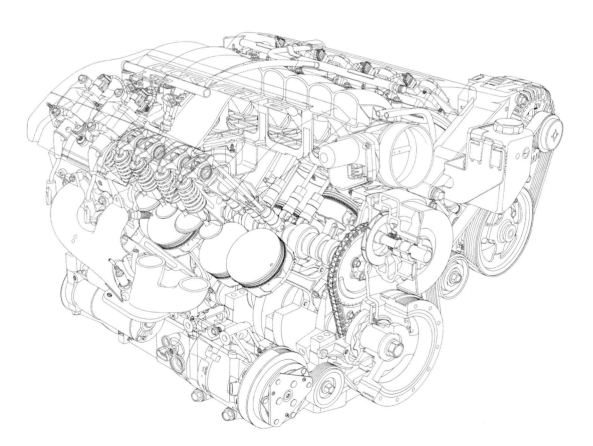

The C6's roller tappets and stronger valve springs, which are similar to those in the LS6 V-8 of the 2004 Corvette Z06, can be seen in this line drawing.

The same 400-horsepower engine lives in both the coupe and convertible models of the 2005 Corvette.

speed is between 12 and 15 miles per hour. Most drivers rarely experience this movement, and cars exported overseas don't get the feature.

In the final design, the new Corvette's fluid pump, coolers, larger torque converter, and gearsets became heavier, requiring weight to be reduced in other parts of the car so that the 2005 Corvette could meet its performance goals. The automatic transmission weighs 195 pounds and the manual weighs 121 pounds. The new torque converter adds slightly more than half a pound. These weights take on tremendous significance when you realize how expensive the Corvette's diet has been: Each pound is worth roughly $5 per car to remove, according to chief engineer Dave Hill, assuming a 30,000-unit annual production.

AUTOMATIC TRANSMISSION

IN THE SUMMER OF 2000, GM'S POWERTRAIN DIVISION began working on a version of the 4L65-E automatic transmission that was going to be used in increasingly more powerful vehicles, including the 2005 Corvette. Part of that development included designing more durable gearsets. The gearsets would not only be used on the sixth-generation Corvette, but also on GM trucks, and they would offer a broad menu of final drive ratios.

In the development process, they became five-pinion planetary gearsets, the added pinions giving the gearset more strength to survive with the higher-torque engine. To reduce friction so that the gearsets can operate at high speeds, the washers between them are made of Teflon. While the Dex111 fluid used to lubricate the transmission is still rated for a 100,000-mile life, GM recommends a 50,000-mile change if the car is being driven hard or raced regularly. The C6's automatic transmission has a standard 2.73:1 final drive, while an optional performance ratio of 3.15:1 is available for quicker acceleration and is also standard on Z51-equipped cars and European models.

Although the Corvette's four-speed automatic transmission may sound basic, the new car has unique state-of-the-art electronics in the form of a performance shift algorithm, a feature that automatically selects the optimal gear for high-performance driving such as hard cornering. Under these driving conditions, the transmission shifts at higher rpm to provide the car greater responsiveness and flexibility. The performance shift algorithm makes driving the automatic-equipped car easier, and it's a feature that's almost essential in autocross events and race driving.

The performance shift algorithm gathers information—such as throttle movement speed and degree, lateral acceleration, and other functions—from the body and transmission computers, and then it analyzes how quickly the driver wishes to go. During maximum braking or cornering, the transmission automatically downshifts at the moment of opportunity that a skilled driver would downshift a manual transmission. During moderate cornering, the PAS system downshifts more readily when the driver depresses the throttle pedal. High levels of braking, cornering, and acceleration prompt the

Above: **The top view of the engine shows the new composite intake manifold between the two valve covers.**

The aluminum block engine of the new Corvette is sand cast with temperature-controlled cooling to ensure strength. This design also was used in the LS1 V-8.

The alternator, power steering pump, and air conditioning compressor are bolted directly to the block, eliminating brackets that can vibrate and make the car noisier.

transmission to select the lowest gear possible without over-revving the engine, and upshifts occur at the redline speed of the engine. A new valve body spacer allows engine braking, which will occur in the first three gears when the shift lever is in the D3 position.

Part of the team's search for every advantage in efficiency led engineers to use a larger, 300-millimeter torque converter, another upgrade from the 2004 car. It's a heavier unit, but it has a round section shape that's inherently more efficient. This change is one of few in the driveline that actually adds weight, but the benefits include a slight increase in efficiency.

To cool the automatic transmission, a four-plate high-performance oil cooler is attached to the radiator. Additionally, to keep the engine cooler during hard driving, the computer that signals shift functions and torque converter lock-up functions is programmed for a "hot mode." If the fluid reaches 197 degrees Fahrenheit, the torque converter remains locked, except briefly during shifts. This prevents fluid shear in the torque converter from adding heat to the transmission. The more robust torque capacity of the transmission allows higher shift speeds (up to 6,400 rpm) compared to C5, which permitted 6,100-rpm shift speeds.

One of the reasons the sixth-generation Corvette continues to use the front-engine/rear-drive layout is that the transmissions are mounted to the rear differential instead of the engine, and the team felt that this setup provides the best balance for a sports car. The rear differential in the C6, however, uses a new aluminum and iron housing with a new mounting system. Two large wings extend from the top of the housing, and they reduce noise and vibration compared to the single mount of the C5.

Although the transmission is in the rear, the clutch on manual cars and the torque converter on automatic cars are mounted to the engine, and a driveshaft inside of a torque tube carries power back to the transmission and rear differential assembly. The differential is also one of few in the GM lineup that is a combination of aluminum and cast-iron case. Inside the differential, the ring and pinion gears for all 2005 Corvettes are double shot peened, a technique that strengthens the metal and ensures that the gears will handle the increased torque of the LS2 engine. Previously, this process was done on the C5 Corvette only for the LS6-equipped Z06 model.

The greater output of the powertrain led the Corvette team to think of better ways to get that power to the road, and new technologies were developed to do that.

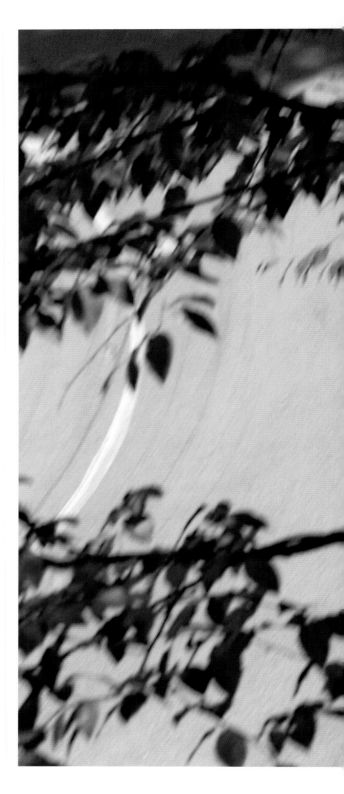

The sixth-generation Corvette still uses the front-engine/rear-drive layout because the development team thought this setup, where the transmission is mounted to the rear differential instead of the engine, provides the best balance for a sports car.

Above and opposite: **Even with a more aerodynamic shape and a more powerful engine and driveline system that could produce more power, the 2005 Corvette still needed upgrades in technology to reach its top speeds.**

Some of the sophisticated technology used in the sixth-generation Corvette includes electronic controls that monitor and control the driver-induced forces on the tires, a central computer-controlled operating system, and advanced handling systems, which all rely on each other to work properly.

Four

Twenty-First Century Technology

Advanced Electronics Make the C6 a High-Tech Leader of the Pack

"We already have a car that satisfies a large percentage of customers, now we have more technical knowledge. Now we can make it unexpectedly better."

—Dave Hill, chief engineer and vehicle line executive for the Corvette

THE SIXTH-GENERATION CORVETTE DEPENDS heavily on new technology, twenty-first century technology, to accomplish its ambitious performance mission. Much of this technology was in its infancy when GM engineers and designers first tackled the 2005 Corvette project, but now the upgrades are crucial to the car's increased dynamic capability and its design.

For example, the run-flat, or EMT, tires on the new Corvette cannot be used on the car without sophisticated electronic controls monitoring and controlling the driver-induced forces on the tires. In turn, the electronic controls depend completely on the new electrical system that connects and signals all of the car's computer-controlled operating systems, and that system is essential for the advanced handling systems, such as the F55 magnetic selective ride control, to work.

ELECTRONICS

A 2005 CORVETTE HAS MUCH IN COMMON with a local area network of office computers that transmits data in real time. The Corvette's high-tech electronic system is

With all these new components, there is no wasted space under the fiberglass skin of the 2005 Corvette.

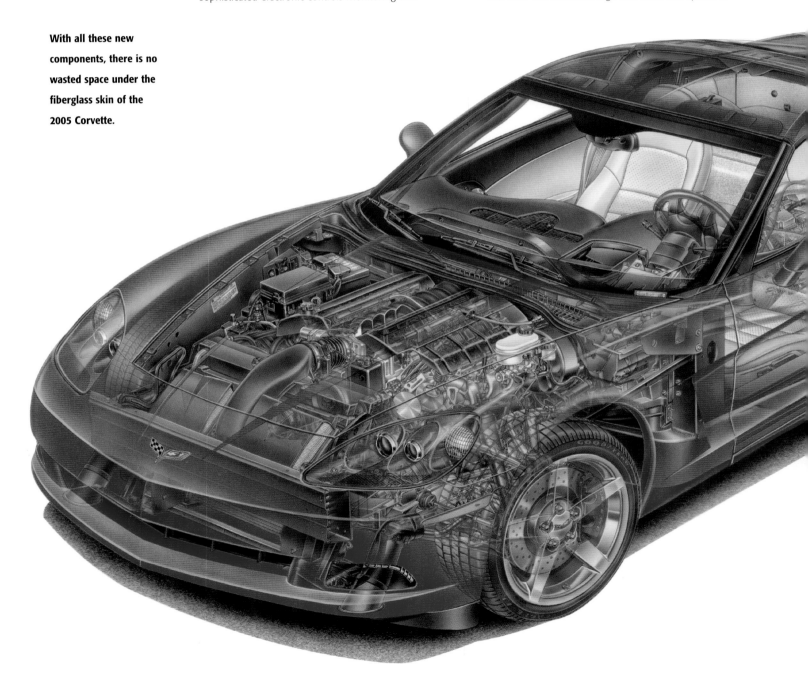

The EMT (run flat) tires needed to be redesigned for the car to improve its ride quality, so engineers and designers used a different rubber compound that would still withstand higher temperatures.

David Kimble

powered by 17 computers, which are connected in the 2005 Corvette by a network cable running through the central body control module (BCM). All of the computers instantaneously control a variety of functions, such as anti-lock braking and stability control, and they communicate just a few milliseconds slower for functions such as operating door switches, mirror controls, and lock/security systems. Stan Modjeski, the vehicle systems engineer responsible for all of the electronics, says, "The data that shows what the car is doing—in terms of speed, steering angle, relative acceleration, wheelspin, attitude, and driveline health—is constantly circulating on this high-speed cable, ready for any function that the car needs."

For instance, when you press a window switch, it doesn't send current to the window motor, but instead the switch signals a request to the BCM to lower the window, and it directs the current. The advantage to this is that other functions, such as the electric convertible top, will know when the windows are down or up. Eventually, most GM cars will be wired like this for smart components, but the Corvette is leading the way toward this electrical plan.

Because the car's electronics control power delivery, the accelerator pedal is no longer physically connected to the engine. A small motor operates the throttle, so the accelerator pedal is an electronic position switch. "I care a lot about how much torque I get if I press a gas pedal; I don't want it snapping on and off," Corvette engineer Dave Zimmerman says. "In the old days, you had a cam

The double-A arm front suspension on the new Corvette has improved the ride of the car. The aluminum control arms in the system help keep unsprung weight to a minimum.

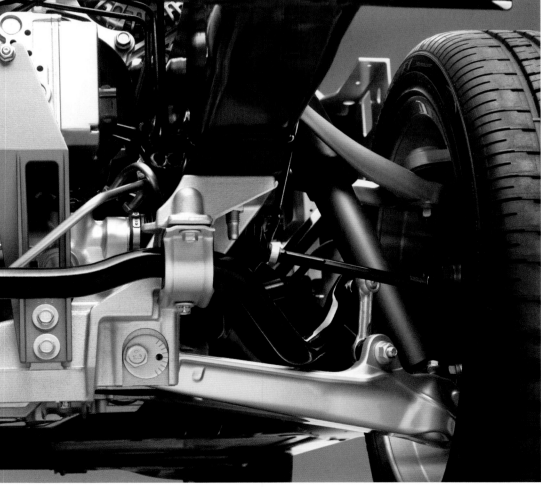

The rear suspension is also a double-A arm design, which has been modified from the fifth-generation Corvette's.

and levers and you had a train of linkage coming at the throttle blade. Then we started doing cables because you can only do certain things with those linkages—you could only turn them in certain directions. With drive by wire, we can do anything we want. You have a very aggressive throttle blade and throttle pedal, and that gives you real snappy performance. People say, 'Wow, feel all this power.' " One benefit of drive by wire is that a driver who is making unnecessary throttle pedal movements won't be wasting fuel.

When the Corvette project started, the team was still crafting the car's high-intensity discharge low-beam headlights. Driven by aerodynamics, styling, and the need for more compact space in the front of the Corvette, those designing the car decided that the headlights would be exposed on the sixth-generation Corvette, even though they've been hidden on the Corvette for more than 40 years. The result is the Corvette's first specific headlight. The new lights use small, high-intensity xenon discharge (HID) low beams and more conventional halogen high

beams in a projector-type reflector. The low beams remain lighted when high beams are selected. European regulations also drove the addition of a headlight washer system, with nozzles that pop up from the front fascia during use.

The new electronics also enabled the car's chassis systems to become more advanced. In 2003, late in the C5 era, engineers pulled forward a major electronic chassis technology that had been destined for the C6—magnetic selective ride control, the world's fastest-reacting damping system. It uses magneto-rheologic shocks, which are filled with a special fluid that contains randomly suspended iron particles. These particles can change the flow properties of the fluid almost instantly according to the level of electric current sent to a magnet in each shock. The end result feels somewhat like a giant hand grabbing a wheel that's hit a big bump, thus controlling its tendency to bounce, yet letting go of the wheel as it rolls on smoother surfaces. Previous "real-time damping" systems used data to adjust a vehicle's shock damping.

For the rear suspension, the lower control arms are mounted to a new subframe.

The by-the-millisecond speed of magnetic selective ride control changed the game.

A computer controls how much current is sent to the shocks. "Now the shock can use the data almost as fast as [the information is] received, and that's the big thing," Modjeski says. The special F55 shocks look the same as conventional Corvette shocks, except they have a wire coming from the top. This system debuted in the 2003 Corvette and continues in the C6 era.

STANDARD ACTIVE HANDLING

EVEN ON CARS NOT EQUIPPED with the magnetic selective ride option, two other electronic systems operate the four brakes on the car in the same way that a conductor leads a quartet. The sophisticated stability system actually helps both the casual driver and the serious sport driver in any condition on the road. "The nice thing about our stability system is at least when you enter into it, it's very subtle," says Dave Zimmerman, the vehicle systems engineer for

the new Corvette chassis. "It helps the driver without over-governing the driving experience."

The system monitors the driver's action through a steering-wheel angle sensor, another car body sensor that works like a gyroscope, and speed sensors. "The system will say, 'I know where the car's going and I know at what rate it's going to change direction, but I know by the way this guy's turning the wheel [that] he wants to turn a lot quicker than what the car really is doing.' And also by the fact he's jammed the brake pedal as close to the floor as he can and he's engaged ABS, he' s got the vehicle beyond his ability to drive it, say like a professional race car driver would be able to," Zimmerman says.

The system learns all of this almost instantly, and its computer is programmed to decide the best way to help the driver, he adds. "What it can do is determine, based on the turn, whether you want to maintain the throttle where it's at or back off the throttle; or, how much do you

The 2005 Corvette's braking performance has moved into exotic car territory in part due to the car's massive 13.4-inch rotors.

want to brake, not only on what side, but on what corner of the vehicle. It will actually put in an additional steering input by using the brakes to pull or push the vehicle through the turn that the driver's trying to do, but is unable to."

When the system is working in a C6 equipped with the F55 magnetic selective ride control, it can also use the variable damping to help change the attitude of the car. "It says, 'I know what the car's doing and I know what the driver is trying to make the car do, but he isn't, so I'll help him up to the limit of the laws of physics,' " Zimmerman explains.

Computers aren't born knowing how to drive cars, however, so every situation is painstakingly created by the

Braking performance on Z51 cars is also enhanced by holes that have been drilled into the rotors to aid cooling.

The signature "David Kimble" appears on the illustration.

The weight of heavy components such as the engine and transmission has been divided between the front and rear axles in the car to better its handling balance.

With the improvements to the tires, they can now still hold air after at least an hour of non-stop high-speed test track driving.

car's chassis engineers on test tracks and public roads and then recorded as software code. Therefore, when Zimmerman says the computer is sensing the condition of the driver and deciding what to do with the car, it's really not an anonymous machine making the decisions. "It's a whole bunch of us," he notes.

SUSPENSION GEOMETRY

IN THE END, THE CAR'S ELECTRONICS ARE LIMITED to the abilities of the suspension pieces themselves, which are the limbs of the car. Their angles and range of motion determine how well the car balances between a tendency to go straight and to turn. The goal of the sixth-generation Corvette, and any high-performance vehicle, is to have both these abilities combined without taking away from either.

Since 1997, the Corvette has been eager to turn on the road, maybe too much so. While this ability makes the car very responsive on the racetrack and on challenging roads, engineers found room for improvement for times when the car is running straight down an interstate highway. To counter that tendency, they made the caster angle of the C6's front suspension greater than what was possible during the era of the C5's design. "But, you can't just change caster," development engineer Mike Neal says. "The design is built around where the wheel is in the wheelhouse. You have to really design for it."

In addition, to better improve the ride of the car, engineers and designers increased the sixth-generation Corvette's suspension travel, giving it longer legs—literally. "We wanted a better riding car and a better handling car. Suspension travel helps both categories," Neal says. Some of the travel came from the tires, which are more apt to envelop small bumps in the road instead of bouncing off them. The internal clearance in the shocks was increased as well, and the steering knuckles were machined for more clearance. In combination, the wheels travel up and down 13 millimeters farther than in the fifth-generation Corvette, and in the chassis-tuning world those millimeters are substantial because most often suspension upgrades are marked in millimeters, not in inches.

"We made a significant change to increase ride travel front/rear, particularly in the rear. Coupled with a tire that's much softer, that's better enveloping—which is also part of your suspension, part of your ride travel—the new Corvette is a lot more comfortable in more places," Neal says. "To get a greater articulation of the suspension, we had to reposition the ball joints so that we wouldn't run out of travel. Then the rear suspension, we took the rear spring—it was hanging below the control arm with the links—and set it up cradled in the control arm like the front suspension of the C5, and that eliminated some parts and made it lighter, stronger, and more cost efficient."

The overall effect of the greater caster angle and other geometry changes improves not just the ride of the car over bumps, but the dynamics of how the car handles and steers. "It's going to be less touchy; it's going to be less tuggy; it's going to be more poised; it's going to be better isolated; it's not going to read as much stuff in the road; and it's going to be quieter to road noise," Neal says. As to what "less tuggy" means, he says that the Corvette driver won't sense any unnatural pushing or pulling on the car as it follows a tight corner.

The Corvette's new shifter and handbrake fit inside a more rigid center console.

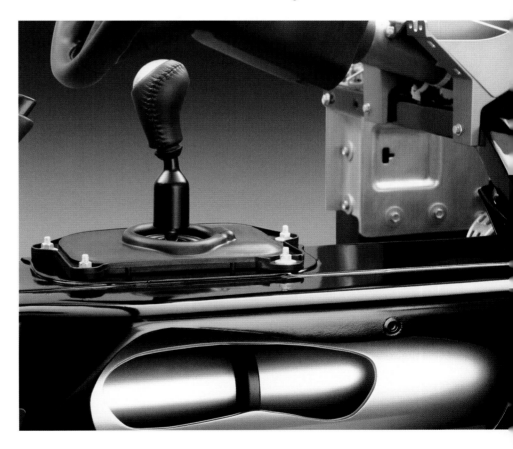

The driveshaft runs inside a torque tube, within the car's center tunnel, from the engine to the transmission.

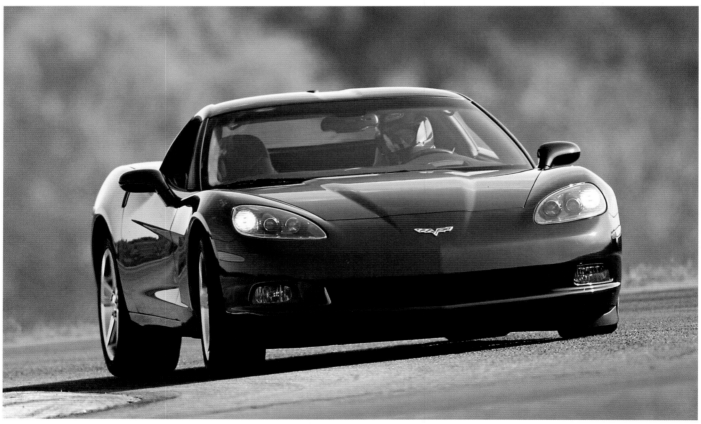

Because the car's electronics control power delivery, the accelerator pedal is no longer physically connected to the engine. A small motor operates the throttle, so the accelerator pedal is just an electronic position switch.

After the C5 was built with one cup holder, engineers and designers knew they had to find a way to squeeze two cup holders into the new Corvette's center console.

Z51 PEFORMANCE PACKAGE

ALTHOUGH THE CALIBRATIONS FOR THE STANDARD 2005 CORVETTE are biased toward performance driving, some Corvette customers still want more racetrack-oriented behavior. Therefore, the three different suspensions available on the new Corvette are intended for different driving styles. "Think about Corvette drivers in a couple of ways—touring and sporting. If they're touring the open road, we tune it so they can go clear across the country and feel great at the end of the day," Neal says. These customers are directed toward the standard and the F55 magnetic selective ride control suspensions.

"But we also have customers who want the ability for track-ready performance." For those drivers, the sixth-generation Corvette sports the Z51 suspension, which comes with the Z51 Performance Package. The Z51 takes the 2005 Corvette closer to being a race car, with firmer springs and shocks, stiffer anti-roll bars, and more aggressive tires. All four brake rotors are larger and cross drilled in this package; the front rotors are 0.6 of an inch larger in diameter, and the rear rotors measure an inch larger in diameter. The cheeks of the rotor are thicker, although the overall thickness of the Z51 rotors remains the same. The rotors are about eight pounds heavier than the biggest C5 rotors, one of the few areas that a weight gain was allowed with the C6. But the extra stopping performance, feel, and durability were deemed major priorities.

EMT TIRES

BETTER HANDLING PERFORMANCE IS ALMOST ALWAYS achieved with larger wheels and tires. As wheels and tires grow larger and wider, the problem of carrying a spare tire is magnified, and that's why the fifth-generation Corvette was unique with its extended-mobility tires (EMT), known as run-flat tires, which eliminate the need to carry a spare and jack. Corvette and longtime supplier Goodyear pioneered EMT technology in the early 1990s-era fourth-generation Corvettes. The formula was revised for the C5 and again for the C6. "We're the only car in the world to now have the advantage of three generations of run-flat tires," chief engineer Dave Hill says. "And again we have, with Goodyear, achieved a major improvement."

The calibrations for the standard 2005 Corvette are biased toward performance driving, but for customers who want more racetrack-oriented behavior in their C6, they can choose the Z51 Performance Package. The Z51 takes the 2005 Corvette closer to being a race car, with firmer springs and shocks, stiffer anti-roll bars, and more aggressive tires.

As a result, if you grip the sidewall on the new Corvette's tires, the thick rubber can't be moved. This is part of what enables the tires to run up to 100 miles without any air pressure inside. "So we're using rubber compounds that can stand higher temperature and all that, and still be softer," Zimmerman says. The run-flat tires on the fifth-generation car were capable of exceeding 200 miles without any air pressure, and the team decided that was an unnecessarily long distance to travel before stopping for service or repair. Extensive research from more than a decade of experience found that improving the run-flat ride characteristics and performance was far more important to drivers than maximizing zero-pressure driving range.

Easing up the requirement for the tires to go at least 200 miles without any air pressure allowed Goodyear to design the tires to have more traction, as well as absorb small bumps better and run more quietly. In addition, the

Corvette's stability system also reacts when there's a flat tire: "Normally, we don't want to be intrusive and take the fun out of spirited driving with our active-handling philosophy, so we don't. So we have a double calibration that recognizes a flat. Then we introduce more aggressive active-handling calibration. If it's off, it's automatically turned on. That keeps the driver from trying to slide on an exit ramp with a flat," Zimmerman says.

The standard tires have tread blocks that are directional, while the Z51 tires have an asymmetric tread pattern. "The asymmetric tires have outside tread blocks that are designed for dry and inside tread blocks [that] are designed for wet. In addition, we want to improve the wet performance of today's tire, and although today's (C5) tire is not really considered an all-season tire at all—and the C6 is not either—we wanted to make it proficient in wet conditions as well. They did improve wet weather traction somewhat," Neal says.

In the tire world, the improvements are significant, especially considering that the sidewall height of the new Corvette's tires is shorter than the same dimension on C5 tires. Yet the C6 tires do have a wheel diameter that's an inch larger. The bigger wheel created the opportunity for larger brakes to fit inside for the Z51 Performance Package. Overall rolling resistance of the stickier tires stays the same as the C5's tires, but friction reductions in the rest of the C6 drivetrain resulted in the new car having less rolling resistance overall, which aids fuel efficiency.

SAFETY

THE SAFETY EXPERTS WON'T BE DISAPPOINTED in the sixth-generation Corvette, even in its convertible form. "We've actually gone beyond the federal requirement by having convertibles actually exceed the standard for a coupe," says Dorian Tyree, vehicle integration engineer for safety.

And although the C6 became smaller and lighter than the C5, the Corvette's safety wasn't compromised, Tyree adds. New features include dual-stage air bags and seatbelt pretensioners. Getting all that new equipment into the new car added complexity, testing, and development time. Because of the changes, the team conducted 45 crash tests for the new Corvette, a more than 50-percent increase from those conducted for the fifth-generation car.

If you get behind the bumper of the new Corvette and take a close look at the metal plates where the

engine hood attaches, you'll see even more evidence of pieces that have been added to improve crash performance. A front-frame reinforcement pulls double duty as a hood hinge brace, but its mission is to slow the bending of the frame rail in the event of a frontal crash. "When you shorten up the car, you actually reduce the time the car has to absorb energy. The stiffer frame compensates by actually absorbing more energy," Tyree

says. Another piece was added inside the bumper rail, a thin strip of corrugated sheet metal to keep the bumper square as it begins to crush in a collision. "This is what we call a bumper stuffer," he says.

"One thing we can't do in the virtual world very well [is] predict the fuel tank crash performance using just an analytical model. The fifth generation's fuel system is a wonderful one, but with the sixth generation we've made

The traditional sports car cockpit also features high-tech electronics, such as satellite navigation and a head-up gauge display. The screen in the center of the console displays radio and climate information or data from the optional navigation system.

some improvements." The two plastic fuel tanks in the Corvette are connected by a rubber cross-over hose in the C5, but for the sixth-generation Corvette designers and engineers decided to use a stainless-steel hose. An added bonus is that the new hose is easier to install during assembly.

Part of the car's improved occupant protection comes in the form of side air bags—an optional feature on the new coupe and standard on the convertible—and improved, standard front air bags. The standard front air bags are a new dual-stage type, which deploy at reduced force during a severe impact should a small person be seated or when an impact is not as severe. A manual on/off switch has also been added that can disable the passenger air bag in the event small children are along. The car also has a seatbelt retractor system that "actually

A new configurable driver information display sits between the new Corvette's large gauges.

The uplevel audio system has a CD changer in the dash instead of the trunk.

pulls the seat belt down," Tyree says. The retractor deploys with the first stage of the front air bag system. The retractor is mounted on the roof bar bow on coupes and on a casting that is mounted to the seat mounting on convertibles. A new computer module controls the functions and has its own power supply, should the battery become disconnected during a crash.

THE AUDIO SYSTEM

RACETRACK PERFORMANCE IMPROVEMENTS weren't the only upgrades the development team focused on in its revamping of the Corvette. The team knew that long-distance cruising also is a passionate endeavor for Corvette customers, and such road treks provide an opportunity to appreciate a top-notch audio system.

Part of that system includes a standard, stereo CD player that will play MP3-coded discs and an optional Bose stereo system with a six-CD changer in the instrument panel. The Bose system also has a feature called Audio Pilot. It includes a microphone that detects rain, surrounding traffic, or wind, and then signals the system to compensate by changing the tone of the audio for each of the different noise levels. It will also compensate for the wind noise in the convertible when the top is down. When the optional navigation system is installed, the map display screen doubles as a touch-screen for the controls of the radio.

For days when the sun is shining brightly, the 2005 Corvette has been outfitted with plastic lenses over the

Above: **The lower black panel is called a diffuser and helps air to exit from under the body.**

New, smaller high-intensity light technology allowed the exposed headlight systems to fit within the 2005 Corvette's fenders.

To provide more rollover protection, the new Corvette's windshield frame is designed to hold the same weight as a fixed roof.

radio display and the climate-control display that are angled so reflections from the sun won't reflect into a driver's eyes. In addition, the lenses have a microscopic coating that will cut reflections and glare, similar to professional quality camera lenses and some eyeglasses. "This is something that's very high tech; it's only in use on two other cars than I'm aware of," says Todd Fast, the interior systems engineer for the Corvette. "The Lexus

SC430 has it, and that was used as our benchmark for display readability." Cadillac's DeVille sedan also uses a similar coating.

Bose audio systems are also capable of receiving XM satellite radio, as well as satellite-based navigation and GM's OnStar services. Because of these capabilities, the 2005 Corvette has three satellite antennae. The XM satellite audio antenna is on the rear roof bow, ahead of

the glass hatchback, and looks like a small, upside-down row boat. On convertibles, this antenna is on the trunk lid. The optional navigation antenna goes on the inside of the windshield in front of the mirror, and the OnStar antenna also sits on the windshield to the right of the mirror. The normal AM/FM antenna is a large foil disc hidden under the plastic body of the car. "It looks like a pizza," Modjeski says. "Little Caesar's large."

With the complex radio station information available, the team wanted a head-up display to be available so drivers concentrating on the road could see the dashboard better. The HUD is a new reconfigurable display, which allows the alpha-numeric digits to change size. Normally the display features a digital speedometer prominently, but when you change radio stations, for example, the station number is briefly displayed next to

Right: **Countless detail improvements combine for a high-quality interior on the sixth-generation Corvette, including a more comfortable seat, a better designed steering wheel, and a top-notch shifting knob for the manual transmission.**

Below: **In place of a conventional ignition switch, this button starts the engine with a single push.**

the speedometer number, which momentarily shrinks in size. In addition, the head-up display has a street mode and a track mode. In track mode, the turn signal and high-beam indicators disappear, while the tachometer and the g-meter are displayed largely. In street mode, the driver can choose the speedometer with tachometer readings, radio information, and even navigation system directions to be displayed.

The radio and air-conditioning displays are positive-mode LCD. "Dave Hill wanted the LCD display because its readability is enhanced by sunlight," Fast says. Previous Corvette displays were vacuum fluorescent, which are harder to read in direct sunlight. The driver information center (DIC) in the instrument panel has a sharper image and can carry more data. It is powered by an organic light emitting diode (OLED), which is a brighter display in sunlight and recently has been used in newly popular digital camera cell phones. The new DIC also has a two-line alpha-numeric display that can be personalized with the car owner's name, display trip information, oil life, tire pressures, as well as the status of programmable features such as passive locking.

KEYLESS ACCESS WITH PUSH-BUTTON START
BECAUSE THE NEW ELECTRICAL SYSTEM enables computer-controlled functions, the old-fashioned metal key has been rendered obsolete, replaced by electrons. The car unlocks and prepares to start when two sets of sensors locate a transmitter that is continuously transmitting a code. So the new Corvette doesn't have conventional door handles. Small pockets behind the rear edges of both doors and the rear hatch contain pressure sensitive pads; fingers touching this pad signal each door to unlatch. If the sensors have found the transmitter near the door, or inside the car, the door will unlatch. Once the driver has entered the car, interior sensors look for the same transmitter. When it is found to be inside the car, the driver can press a rocker switch on the instrument panel to start the engine.

In manual transmission cars, the clutch pedal must be depressed before the car will start, and in an automatic car, the brake pedal must be depressed before starting. This feature prevents a passenger from starting the car. The new Corvette can also be programmed to lock the doors automatically (passive locking) if desired.

Another thing that makes the car harder to break into is its electronic latch mechanism, located in the B-pillar of the car, not inside the door. "There are no mechanical lock rods, so you can't use one of those crowbar things; there's nothing to hit inside the door," Modjeski says. Each door also has a small, flashing red LED where a conventional lock knob would be to let outsiders know the door is locked. Export models have redundant deadbolts, a theft prevention requirement in some European countries.

To pop open the rear hatch, a sensor similar to those on the doors is below the license plate. In the unlikely event of a total power failure, the car has a conventional key that will open the rear hatch, and a hidden cable release inside the rear cargo area will open the doors.

THE REST OF THE INTERIOR
CORVETTE ENTERS THE CUP HOLDER WARS with the 2005 model. The team decided that two cup holders should be built into the center console for the sixth-generation Corvette, and those cup holders should be designed so that a Coke bottle would not tip over in a 1.0-g corner. "The original target was to try to meet a 1.0-g requirement for lateral and fore/aft stability," says Fernando Krambeck, vehicle systems engineer for the interior of the car. The depth of the cup holders proved crucial to reach the goal.

Longer bottom cushions provide more comfort while higher side bolsters support occupants better during spirited driving.

The Corvette team also wanted to make the Corvette's seats more comfortable and offer more support for the occupants. "The way we did that was by taking the side wings on the seat and extending them higher so you get more support higher up on your back," Fast says. "We definitely provided more support up to the shoulder area, whereas the fifth-generation Corvette basically stops down at your lower ribs."

Another area improved to add support was the "halo" in the seats. The halo is a ring around the center of the seat cushion. While it was made firmer, the center—called an insert—stayed softer to keep the seat comfortable. The team also improved the sport seat option. In the C5, the sport seat option had dual lumbar and side wing adjustments, while the sixth-generation Corvette has a seat design with or without single lumbar and side wing adjustments, as well as perforated leather. It comes with or without side air bags. The C6 seat cushion was lengthened as well to give more leg support.

The Corvette team also redesigned the car's interior surfaces and the driver's controls for the C6, including adding a steering wheel that's a slight oval instead of a round disc. "The shape of the section, we feel, better accommodates the human hand," Fast says. In addition, the tilt function for the steering wheel now operates in 2.5-degree increments, twice as fine as that in the C5. Power telescoping of the steering column remains an option.

Topping the shift lever is an oval-shaped knob that designers originally formed out of a clump of body putty. "We worked on that knob for about a year. We wanted something that was more shaped to fit your hand in the different ways that people grab a shift knob. The knob in

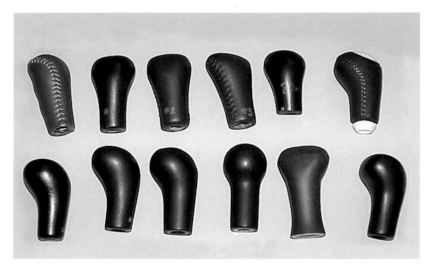

Above: **These dozen shift knobs are some of the designs that were considered for the final knob selection. The 2005 knob is on the left in the photo above and is a smoother shape than the 2004 knob on the right.**

Right: **Here, a variety of drink bottles are checked for clearance from the shift knob and handbrake handle.**

the fifth-generation Corvette looks good, but it doesn't fit your hand," Fast says. In the end, the interior team tested about 20 different knobs and performed blind evaluations to determine the optimal height of the knob. "It turned out to be a very narrow range of what people thought was right, which is good. . . . We ended up with something we all believe is going to be the best shift knob on any moving vehicle."

While coming up with an interior design that was more ergonomic and more functional, the engineers and designers for the new Corvette followed the same philosophy as they did while fine-tuning the car's high-tech chassis and electronics systems: "Eyes on the road, hands on the wheel," Hill reflects. So now it was time to test if that philosophy actually would hold up while driving the car.

This mock-up of a passenger door panel had a moveable grab handle to test for the best location. Below is the final version.

After all the work the Corvette development team put into designing and engineering the car, it was time to see if the C6 lived up to GM's expectations.

Taking It to the Track and Road

Testing, Testing, Testing To Bring the Corvette to Perfection

"The C5 drives bigger, but the C6 drives a lot tidier. It feels lighter on its feet. Its turn-in is quicker. It's very well-balanced."

—Matt DeLorenzo,
Road & Track magazine

EVELOPING THE SIXTH-GENERATION CORVETTE happened in two places: inside, at a high-powered computer screen filled with finite element analyses, and outside, on the road, track, and even on ice-covered grass fields of GM's proving grounds. While cars can be wired with sensors that give engineers data on how quickly the components are working and how hot the car's parts are getting, engineers often rely on what is the best way to test these factors—they drive the car over and over again.

"Seat-of-pants test driving is more important than other testing because that's what the customer experiences. For the finer points of tuning, the human is still the most sophisticated instrument. That's what the customer feels," says Dave Wickman, ride and handling coordinator for the Corvette.

In fact, the first step in the creation of the sixth-generation Corvette began with such a test drive. In 1999, long before there were any C6s, those Corvette team members behind the C5 took about a dozen of them, some Z06 models, on a long road trip. They made notes and brainstormed about what they wanted to improve. Almost unanimously, they decided that the performance and response of the future standard Corvette needed to reach the roaring Z06 race-bred model.

ALPHA AND BETA PROTOTYPES

THESE PRELIMINARY PLANS EVENTUALLY TURNED into reality, becoming "alpha" cars. These alpha cars were basically modified fifth-generation Corvettes, using some drivetrain components intended for the 2005 Corvette. Eventually, engineers and designers added the car's redesigned

suspension pieces and its new 400-horsepower engine. These "mules," however, didn't sport the sixth-generation Corvette's new shape, as the new bodies were still on the drawing board.

Finally, after two years of refining and reshaping the C6 design and testing these mules, the Corvette team produced about 50 "beta" prototypes, still all handmade versions of the car that were much closer to what the final product would be. More than half of these eventually met their end against a crash performance test barrier.

For the C5, most of the beta development drives were conducted on GM's Milford, Michigan, proving ground, a city-sized campus with hundreds of miles of private roads that try to mimic road conditions all over the United States. For the sixth-generation Corvette, the team took the cars off these roads and onto the racetrack,

While testing on the autobahn, the cars were evaluated for real-world driving challenges such as traffic and weather conditions.

The autobahn was the only public road that the Corvette team tested the development cars on where there was no speed limit.

This Nürburgring sticker on the rear window of one C6 development car remained as a badge of honor, despite the fact that the German racetrack testing was long over when this photo was taken.

including Germany's famed Nürburgring, Virginia International Raceway, the Pahrump Speedway outside of Las Vegas, and the small club tracks of Grattan and Gingerman raceways in western Michigan.

In the end, the 14-mile long Nürburgring circuit outside of Cologne, Germany, was the most grueling track where the team tested new Corvette prototypes. "There are maybe four places on the track where you get airborne and you're over 100 miles per hour on every corner," Mike Neal says, adding that it only takes eight laps flat-out before a car is out of fuel. "The Nürburgring is great because it's like wide open country roads versus your table-smooth racetracks."

On the small road course at the desert proving grounds, the Corvette development cars reached 115-mile-per-hour speeds on the short straightaway.

"Track testing is the extreme," Neal adds. "We ran the new Corvette through what we call our high-speed validation program. We choose various tracks for various things. Some tracks present a real challenge in the area of braking, and then our real challenge in most areas is roll control. Some tracks present a challenge for ride control, shock tuning, and stuff like that."

Throughout the process of developing and validating the car, members of the team also took the beta cars out on real road trips almost every month. Later on, those drives spread from Phoenix to southern Ohio and then on to West Virginia. "We had Pinkerton security to make sure no spy photographers came out at night trying to take the car covers off. Photographers have been caught doing that on our drives," Neal says.

One place secluded from those nosy photographers served as a perfect place to test the most complicated and intricate inner workings of the sixth-generation Corvette: GM's expansive desert proving grounds area outside of Phoenix. It has a three-mile-long, high-speed banked track and a "vehicle dynamics road course," which is laid out like a small racetrack. Here, engineers conduct hot-weather testing all year, attaching thermocouples to nearly every moving part of the car. Each of the dozens of tests uncovered a few bugs that still needed to be ironed out in the new Corvette. For example, on one winter test in 2003, Neal wasn't happy with how the car handled when it was fitted with the Goodyear production tires that the team had chosen. Other team members found that the car's rear axle joints and shafts were heating up too much, its transmission fluid was running hot, and the rear diffuser was melting. The exhaust also had a problem—it was making a metallic sound in addition to the deep tone Corvettes are famous for.

To arrive at the suspension calibrations for the car that promised better handling and a smoother ride, the team tested about 50 different tire constructions and about 100 different shock absorber settings in Phoenix and at the Michigan proving grounds. One of Neal's jobs was to select the tires that would work best, both for the sixth-generation Corvette's standard suspension, the F55

magnetic ride, and for the Z51 Performance Package. Since the Z51 promises racetrack competence, he had to drive the tires back-to-back on different racetracks, as well as on the proving ground road courses. After this grueling process, Neal determined that his favorite Z51 performance tire was made of a "D" compound, a combination of different mold constructions. He decided to go with the tires made of an early mold construction because they offered the best consistency and grip. He also thought the tires felt good to him through the steering wheel.

He and other members of the Corvette team also conducted high-speed testing at both proving grounds' closed racetracks. "We begin by going to Black Lake (an acre asphalt pad on the proving grounds) and setting up a challenge course and running 250 miles," he explains. "We prove it there first, then we go to the racetrack and do a 24-hour test. It isn't one day; it's 24 hours of lap time. That's basically six days of running. So we don't count the time when we're in the pits, changing oil, tires, drivers, and stuff like that. Then the third test is what we call our maximum velocity test, so that's wide-open throttle at the highest velocity the car will run, which is actually in fifth, not sixth gear, right at redline. The new car's going to be faster than the old car, and we've tested over 180 miles per hour. The steering in the old car at top speed was fairly light. This car, with our new aerodynamics, is more solid and confidence inspiring—even at very extreme conditions."

KEEPING THE NEW CORVETTE SAFE AND MANAGEABLE

DURING THIS TESTING, THE TEST DRIVERS have to make sure the car is manageable by the average driver at the sixth-generation Corvette's high levels of performance. "We have to really do a lot of unnatural acts and do the things that put the car in a position that could potentially happen and you hope that nobody would ever have to do, like a 135-mile-per-hour accident avoidance maneuver," Wickman says. "And in a maneuver like that, we make sure that if the driver does something with the brakes or with the throttle to upset the car, he's still OK."

Test drive chief Mike Wickman speaks to electrical engineer Stan Modjeski during a winter drive on rural back roads.

Despite the chill, chief engineer Dave Hill is happy with how well the winter test driving of the development cars is going in 2003.

This page and opposite:
Testing the car on the racetrack or the road is not about making it faster, but about making it safer for drivers.

The white development car saw lots of track action at the Nürburgring race course in Germany and in the United States.

Keeping the driver safe is only one concern the team has to address, though. Wickman notes that he wants the car to handle and accelerate like a performance car even on snow and ice. He and other Corvette engineering team members tested the car to reach this objective at GM's testing facility in Michigan's Upper Peninsula, where there is a 300- by 3,000-foot ice pad. "We took the sixth-generation Corvette out here and did evasive maneuvers at 60 miles per hour," he says. "In terms of traction control calibrations for ice, there's a tradeoff between the stability and acceleration. So, we're out here looking for the acceleration that this vehicle

needs, but still keeping the driver in command. We're trying to minimize throttle intervention."

"We didn't come out to the track to try to make the car go faster. We go to the track to do the extreme. Situations the driver may never get himself in. People who haven't driven performance cars much, you would like a measure of safety for them, as much as you can, but you don't restrict the guy who wants to drive the car. We're allowing him to have fun."

Corvette's consistent legacy and continuous improvement is a huge advantage in accomplishing that, says Hill, chief engineer. For example, the new Ford GT

Above: **On an unusually warm day during winter testing, calibration engineer Mike Petrucci checks the stability calibrations on this recently uncamouflaged Corvette development car.**

Left: **The "track" where the car is tested for snow traction and handling really is just a large grass field that's green most of the year, not white.**

was developed with no predecessor in a short period of time, and therefore doesn't have the benefits that the C6 has received during its thorough optimization process, he says. "We suspect this Ford GT is going to be a fairly heavy piece, around 3,400 pounds," Hill said in late 2003. "It could be hundreds of pounds heavier than the [2006] Z06 model. That's the trouble when you don't have an existing baseline car to start from and you've got a high price and small sales volume. We have a major advantage in terms of thoroughness. We go after every tenth of an ounce. For completely new projects, like a GT, they may have to overdesign with excess mass to have a built-in safety factor. That's a very daunting task. With Corvette, we had a fifth generation that we know everything about—the good and the not-so good. We reach a level of fine-tuning that reaches an extremely minute level. [Ford has] overdone a lot of areas just to get it together so quickly."

By the amount of time the group took to refine the C6, Wickman is confident that the 2005 Corvette is a very fine-tuned product. He and the rest of the Corvette team are even more confident because GM wants to win another first-place J. D. Power and Associates Initial Quality Survey for the sixth-generation 'Vette. And that will be possible, in large part, due to the diligence of those putting the car together at GM's Corvette plant in Bowling Green, Kentucky.

The test drivers count the deserted dirt roads near General Motors' northern Michigan test facility as some of their favorites to use during development testing.

Petrucci takes a break during a winter development test.

The Nürburgring track is 14 miles long and very difficult to learn, according to most racing drivers familiar with competing on the circuit.

Places on the track will launch a car traveling at high speed into the air, though test driver Mike Neal says the landing in the new Corvette is soft.

The 2005 Corvette was tested in every condition and every climate to ensure that the car will be a top performer even in slick conditions.

Maneuverability and ride comfort is also a priority for those Corvette customers who prefer boulevard cruising.

This camouflaged development car is being driven in a 24-hour track test at Grattan raceway. The test is really a week-long event because the 24 hours counts only lap time, not breaks, driver changes, or vehicle maintenance.

Here, the track testing focuses on improving the Corvette's Z51 Performance Package with upgraded suspension, tires, and brakes.

During testing drivers evaluated wind noise and turbulence inside the cockpit of the Corvette convertible. They also monitored the car's top performance and chassis rigidity.

The test drivers credit the sixth-generation Corvette's new tires for offering a higher level of slick road handling and traction while driving.

The team tried to use desolate roads as mush as possible, but camouflaged bodies kept the Corvette's final shape hidden from an ever-curious public.

Track performance was a priority for the Z51 Performance Package option—an option that is still comfortable for a Corvette driver who prefers everyday street driving.

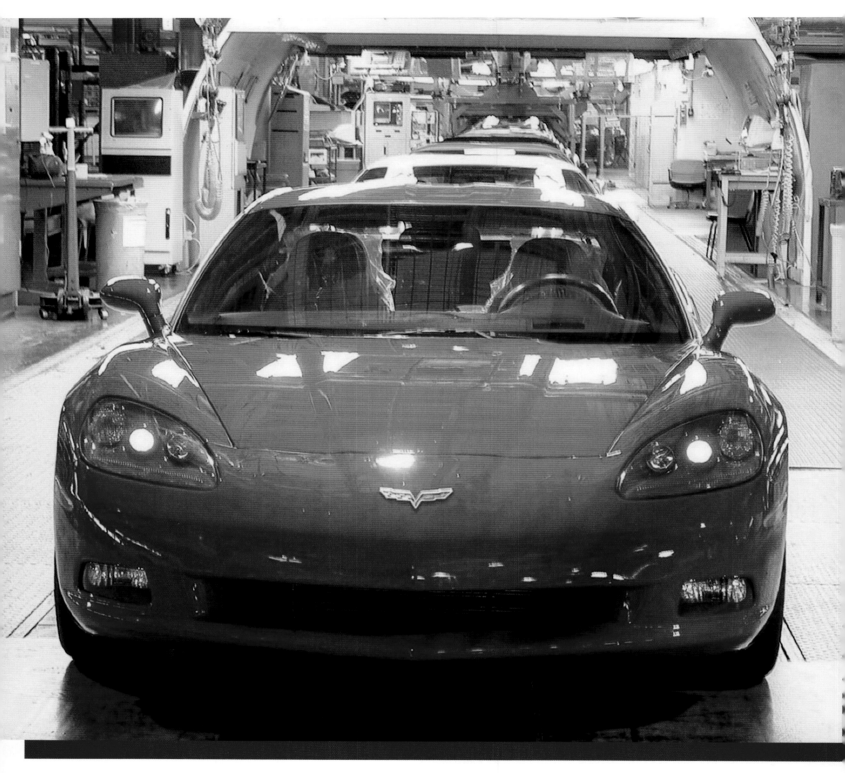

The first 2005 Corvettes come off the assembly line and await testing in Bowling Green, Kentucky.

Six

Building It Right in Kentucky

Highly Trained Workers Use the Latest Tools to Put the Car Together

"Something happened at the swinging Bowling Green bachelor pad of America's favorite sports car, the Corvette. A snooty rich aunt from Cadillac crashed and made herself comfy. But this visitor turned out to be more Auntie Mame than Auntie Em, and her high-class fun-loving ways rubbed off on our hero, who suddenly seems an all-new man."

—Todd Lassa,
Motor Trend, April 2004

QUALITY ISN'T A WORD THAT'S ALWAYS been associated with manufacturing domestic cars, but Corvette manufacturing, particularly at GM's one-million-square-foot facility in Bowling Green, Kentucky, is proving that prejudice wrong. In fact, after quality engineers took precise measurements of many fifth-generation Corvettes in the effort to boost the car's quality and made improvements based upon them, customers responded to the effort. They voted the

A completed C6 in front of the giant fan blades of GM's technical center wind tunnel.

fifth-generation Corvette the world's top premium sports car in the J. D. Power and Associates Initial Quality Survey for 2001 and 2002.

GM executives and members of the Corvette development team want to keep winning these awards, so they have worked hard to make the 2005 Corvette meet and surpass the C5's quality standards. "That's where we're focused and that's where the group is headed, and we've got the tables ready to put the awards on," says quality manager John Reimann.

Aside from initial quality impressions, the Corvette team is going after another J. D. Power award category with the sixth-generation Corvette: perceived quality. "Initial quality is after I've bought the vehicle and I've had it awhile, did it meet my expectations," explains Reimann. "The perceived quality is [about] what is it that captured the customer, where he said, 'I've got to have this car.' One area where we were weak on the perceived quality survey was the interior feel and comfort. And that's where we're focused now.

"It's not so much measuring the gaps for size, but when the customer gets in the car, making sure all the gaps look like they were meant to be the same, equally spaced. It's also got to have the feel of a performance car cockpit, and that's what you've got to go after in that perceived quality. That sometimes gets very, very tough to measure against, but it's the feel of the carpet as well as the surfaces the customer will touch. If you get in there and experience it, you can see there's a big difference between the C5's perceived quality compared to the C6's."

Right now, Reimann notes that his group heavily relies on the autoworkers at the Bowling Green plant to help contain quality issues in the sixth-generation Corvette so the cars can go out to the customer as problem-free as possible. And because those at the plant have seen so many generations of the car, they often know it just as well as engineers and designers. "In most plants they know the current product, they might know some particular features, but when you start talking to the people down at Bowling Green they know the C1 to the C5, all five generations," he adds. "They talk about when the plant started up in 1980 and all the details. They've

got that history of going back to 1953, and it's all
ingrained in each of them, the plant staff, people on the
line. There's passion in everybody down at the plant and
here in engineering; there's just passion behind this car."

Part of that passion has spurred quality engineers to
start addressing more and more of the Corvette's build
variation—where quality issues often arise—into the initial
design of the car. "So if you try to build it wrong, you
won't be able to," he elaborates. "That's why key guys in
the dimensional strategy part work on structure so we can
get the design to reduce build variation between cars. We
can make quality more foolproof in the process."

The process to boost the Corvette's quality first came
in the car's fourth generation, when many 'Vette owners
complained about the car's excessive squeaks and rattles.
To address this, GM executives devoted a special section
of the Bowling Green plant where engineers and
autoworkers could come up with fixes, which included
tightening the car's loose wiring harnesses to keep them
from rattling and filling the fourth-generation Corvette's
body gaps with foam. "On C5 we made a quantum leap
on squeaks and rattles," says dimensional engineer Ron
Kruszewski. "But to think of designing the C6 from scratch
and doing as well as C5 does, that's a great leap."

**A flurry of activity
surrounds the assembly
line for the early C6
manufacturing validation
build (MVB) cars, which
are produced at the
plant to test the
assembly process.**

Engineers and operators at the plant prepare the completed body for the installation of the car's powertrain.

The body is lowered onto the drivetrain, which is mounted on a moving cart that lines up underneath the car's shell.

Since the sixth-generation Corvette uses architecture similar to the fifth-generation car, Kruszewski says that the new Corvette has a head-start in quality. "Now we can refine what we have. There was a refinement we made on the cockpit structure where we went to extruded aluminum instead of cast, and that optimized not only the construction and the build of it, but the fit of the car. Another area we took advantage of was the cockpit structure between the instrument panel, the windshield, the side glass, and the roof panel. That [area] is better than it is on the fifth-generation Corvette, and it will only keep gaining on J. D. Powers' wind, noise, and rattle scores."

An example of engineers and designers changing the car's design to boost quality is the alteration of the sixth-generation Corvette's center console structure. "We linked the console trim plate to the instrument panel center stack. That's always an area in cars that people try to mask for build variation, and we have actually designed that so you not only get the perception that it's right, but it really is right as well."

USING HIGH-TECH TOOLS IN QUALITY CHECK

CHECKING IF A CAR IS "REALLY RIGHT" requires high-tech tools; for example, a laser device measures cut lines between the fascias and the main body of the car. "The challenge on a Corvette is, unlike other cars, that we have two fine-cut lines: the fascia where it meets the rear of the body and the fascia on the front. If you don't have a perfect-length car front to rear, a perfect car, and it's staggered, you will see that imperfection everywhere on the car."

"Now we also have other things in place in the plant, coordinate measuring machines that measure down to 50 microns so we can measure in process as they're building up the car in manufacturing along the way, and we get electronic data," Kruszewski adds. "It's real time now on the Web; we use the Internet to share data. [We] can look at this as fast as these guys can see the car being built in the plant."

He and other quality engineers in Michigan, as well as those working at the Kentucky plant, also use real-time variation video monitors that were in place for the later years of C5 production to verify that the new Corvettes are taking shape correctly. "It watches a piece that's really automated, and with it we can measure how much variation is happening as it goes through its motions. You can't put a person in there, you can't put a tool in there, but we can dynamically watch a station and see if a fixture is adding a variation and why." This equipment detects these variations only when a machine on the assembly line is moving, something not possible to see when the machine has finished its work on the car. Those at the plant are using more of these video monitors for the sixth-generation Corvette than they did with late-model C5s; they also have upgraded the system's technology so that the data collected is animated. The advantage of the animated measurements is that the engineers can see things on moving parts that otherwise look normal if they were not moving.

In all, these video cameras check about 50 dimensions of each sixth-generation Corvette during the assembly process, taking some 129 measurements on the surface of the body and 68 measurements on the interior dimensions of the cockpit. These are checked for variations as small as a sixth of a millimeter, or less than a 100th of an inch. In addition, the coordinate measuring machine (CMM) checks specified points on the body within 50 microns, which is thinner than a human hair.

Some 400 cars were built for testing before the first customer car was built. During this testing, engineers measured whether all of the car's tools and processes were working properly as one unit.

The hydroformed frame technique was created for the C5 and has been modified for the C6 by changing the mounting locations for the new powertrain, cockpit module, and body components.

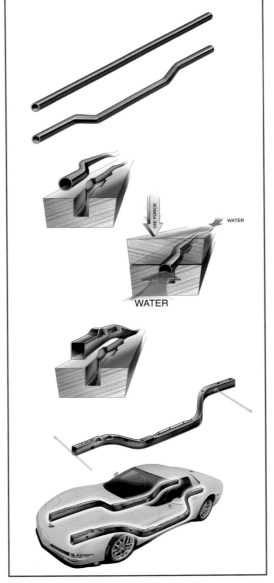

Machines at the plant process the hydroformed frame rails before they're welded together to form the basis of the new Corvette.

MAKING THE PAINT JOB BETTER

THE PAINTING PROCESS FOR THE NEW CORVETTE has also been refined with an eye toward making it a high-quality job. To do this, the car's body panels are painted before the panels are mounted to the car's frame. The 14 panels are painted in racks that are specially designed to take advantage of gravity. In addition, the car's fascias are painted in the same shop, rather than the more common practice of painting fascias off-site by the supplier. This makes it easier to match a car's paint color because of similar shop conditions. These fascias also are first painted with one of three tinted primers (chosen based upon the final color of the car), making the panels' final paint job cover better than if a single gray or white primer had been used.

After painting, the line workers bond the body panels to the car's frame. If they find that there's a flaw in any of the 14 total body pieces, they can replace one piece instead of repainting the entire body. They also have spares for each body part at the plant, in anticipation of a scratch or mark that may occur in the assembly process.

THE TRAINING CENTER

THE STRUCTURE ASSEMBLY OF THE SIXTH-GENERATION CORVETTE gets a similarly high level of attention at the plant. In late 2003, practice assembly stations were set up for each major system of the car. These areas became a training center for assembling the car. About 1,000 employees were trained in the center, although one piece of the technology used wasn't high-tech—an easel board. "Once we start going through this process, every issue gets written on the easel board," Reimann says. "Everything we think is a problem. An easel board system identified 281 issues that were fixed, and that was the precursor to a system to get things fixed when other issues pop up during the build."

Prior to establishing the training center, engineers and line operators from the plant commuted between the plant in Kentucky and the technical center in Michigan for two years, with the priority of making the assembly process part of the design of the car. One way in which they did that was to redesign the fuel transfer system between the car's two fuel tanks. The design they came up with had the transfer pressure lines mounted inside the balance tube between the tanks specifically to make assembly easier. This wasn't the only part designed to be easier to assemble, though. The cockpit structure of the sixth-generation Corvette is 90 percent extruded aluminum, versus about 35 percent extruded for the C5. Extruded parts are easier to locate during the welding process, and they are less vulnerable to variations. The difference is significant since there are about 75 inches of welds on the C6 structure.

"To solve a ride-steer problem on the fifth-generation Corvette, we discovered a frame correction was needed," adds chassis executive Dave Zimmerman. Engineers discovered that the C5's frame was being produced a thousandth of an inch off where the upper front control arms were attached and had to fix this error to get the car to handle exactly the way they wanted. For the new Corvette, monitoring equipment will prevent such errors. Also, the car's windshield frames and door trim panels are designed to fit more precisely.

ON THE ASSEMBLY LINE

WHEN THE CAR IS MOVING on the assembly line, autoworkers make sure the Corvette design process and assembly has come together correctly at various checkpoints. They examine for these five factors:

1) Is there water leakage at the roof?

2) How well does the car's body protect against wind, noise, and penetration?

3) What is the surface appearance of the car?

4) How well do the body panels fit together?

5) And how much effort is required to open the doors, the hatchback, the hood, and the manual convertible top?

This checkpoint process took months to implement at the plant. It began with the assembly of a few C6s, about six months before the first customer car was built. Between then and the time the first customer car rolled off the line, the autoworkers at the Bowling Green plant built 400 Corvettes, 250 of which were given to employees for 90 days to test drive and check for problems.

Powertrain installation is checked on an early MVB car on the assembly line.

A body and frame arrive at the powertrain installation station and are readied for the waiting driveline components.

The engine, driveline, transmission, and differential are installed into the car as a single unit.

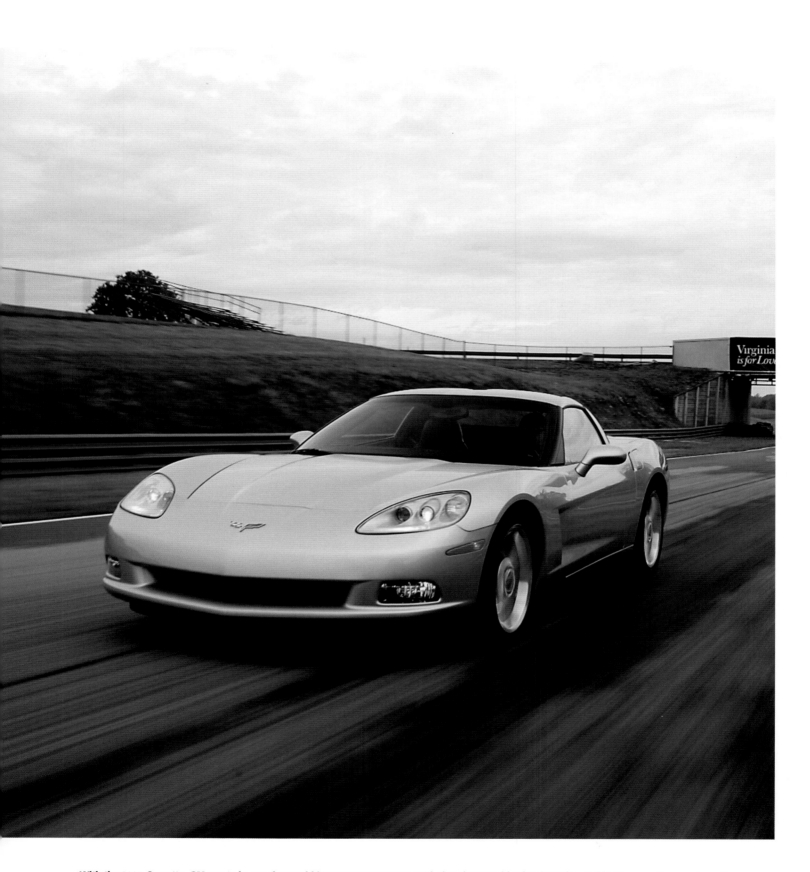

With the 2005 Corvette, GM wanted a car that could impress customers enough that they would select it as the world's top premium sports car in J. D. Power and Associates Initial Quality Survey, just as they did with the C5 in 2001 and 2002.

Part of ensuring that quality includes painting all of the body panels on the 2005 Corvette in the same shop so there are no color variations on the car.

A Family of Flag Ships

The C6 owes part of its newfound refinement to the 2004 Cadillac XLR, which shares its frame architecture with the Corvette and is built in the same plant.

Without the car's new architecture, the 2005 Corvette would likely be a rougher-riding, less-refined car. But thanks to a worldwide boom in luxury roadster popularity in the mid-1990s, and GM's Cadillac division deciding to re-enter the roadster arena, the new Corvette reaped some of the benefits of an even more posh Cadillac XLR architecture.

In 1997, just two years before GM committed to revamping the Corvette, those in the manufacturer's Cadillac division were furiously working on a new image to reverse Cadillac's ailing popularity. As part of that initiative, design boss Wayne Cherry directed the GM studios worldwide to come up with ideas, and one of those ideas included the two-seat Evoq roadster, which was shown at the 1999 Detroit auto show. The concept was a hit, and GM decided that Corvette's sixth-generation rear-drive architecture would be the best platform for the production version of the new Cadillac two-seater.

Hill, who oversaw both the development of the XLR Cadillac and the sixth-generation Corvette, had seen the synergy that would come from building the new Cadillac on the Corvette's architecture. The Cadillac would gain a sportier chassis, and the Corvette plant would be kept busier with another car to build.

To capitalize on the shared foundation, the XLR and the Corvette use the same unique hydroformed frame underneath. "When the frames come out of the primary metal body shop, they're primarily the same structure," structural systems

engineer Ed Moss says. "The Corvette and XLR frames are different just for local attachments such as the top structure."

More shared components include the brackets that attach the dashboard, the front frame reinforcements that are added to improve crash performance, and the new aluminum plate under the center tunnel. To reduce weight in the XLR, the development team used a so-called skid bar in front of the radiator that was aluminum, and the team decided to use this same lighter part in the 2005 Corvette. On the Corvette, the piece has a more complex task than just protecting the radiator if the car drives over an object in the road. "It's got to work right so you can deploy the air bags right, and it's got to protect you in a bumper hit. It was a good accomplishment," Moss adds.

Both cars also share the plastic front air dam, originally developed for the Cadillac. It aids the aerodynamics of the XLR, but is used in the new Corvette because it helps control the car's body lift at the Corvette's higher speeds.

One system that was used first on the 2003 Corvette, and then modified for the XLR, is the sophisticated magneto-rheologic damping system. Due to the range of damping available with the system, the XLR can firm up almost to the level of the Corvette. The calibrations are unique between the cars to preserve their ride characteristics, which are comfort-oriented for the XLR and performance handling–oriented for the Corvette, but the only the Corvette has selectable modes.

Another Corvette refinement, spurred by the requirement to silence the XLR's driveline, is a new mounting system for the rear differential and transmission. Instead of a single bracket, the new mounting system uses two wide arms that sprout from the top of the differential. This system better isolates driveline vibrations from the body of the XLR.

The Cadillac XLR was focused on occupant comfort, which included adding a state-of-the-art

heating and cooling system that would work well with the roadster's convertible top down. Since the new Corvette would also have a convertible offering, the Corvette team was quick to borrow the entire system. The heart of the system includes a smaller, lighter, brushless blower motor that moves as much air as a larger motor. Brushless motors have their electrical windings fixed to the case of the motor, while the magnets rotate within, eliminating the need for any electrical contact to the rotating part of the motor. The design also eliminates the largest source of motor noise, resulting in a much quieter blower. Sophisticated sensors detect the condition of the air inside and outside of the car for temperature, humidity, and for the amount of infrared heat coming from the sun. The goal of these parts is to make the system defog and keep the windows clear in the shortest amount of time and to automatically adjust the climate in the car (with top up or down), even with rapidly changing ambient conditions.

As the team found changes that would make both the XLR and the new Corvette better, the 2005 Corvette became an entirely new car. "We wanted to do sort of the same thing for the XLR, get the wheels farther out also. So it was decided we would start modifying chassis components to do that. Well, now there isn't much that's carryover from the fifth-generation Corvette," Moss adds.

The XLR is powered by the high-tech Northstar multivalve V-8 engine, but it shares its hydroformed frame rails with the Corvette.

huge difference between a luxury roadster and a sports car. All you have to do is drive the two cars and it will hit you like a ton of bricks. They're both two-seat, rear-wheel-drive cars, and that's about where it ends."

One of the big benefits of the Cadillac XLR program was the noise reduction and isolation of vibration, things you wouldn't have normally done to the Corvette because it was not a priority. These changes benefited the Corvette because it was a big priority to Cadillac."

Eventually, a lot more technology upgrades will find their ways into both cars and will be used on other GM cars too. One example of the trickle-down process is apparent in the 2005 Cadillac DeVille sedan. It was developed immediately after the new Corvette and is slicker to the wind because of the shape-tuning techniques aerodynamicist Tom Froling learned while working on the body of the 'Vette. Specifically, the airflow over the front fenders and over and under the tires of the new DeVille improved because of the almost 500 hours of wind tunnel testing Froling did on the Corvette. The new Pontiac GTO coupe, the high-performance Cadillac CTS-V sedan, and the innovative Chevy SSR roadster pickup will gain the drivability improvements from the Corvette's new driveline. Other models are also expected to get the keyless access system and the magnetic ride system.

The first customer-destined XLR rolls off its Bowling Green assembly line in August 2003.

But sizing up the XLR to the Corvette is an apples-and-oranges comparison, says Rick Baldick, marketing director for the Corvette. "The real difference here is, while there's a shared architecture, the XLR is a luxury roadster. There's a

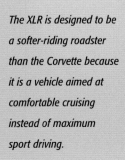

The XLR is designed to be a softer-riding roadster than the Corvette because it is a vehicle aimed at comfortable cruising instead of maximum sport driving.

Right: **Finish quality is hand-checked at the end of the Bowling Green assembly line.**

Below: **Final checks are performed as finished cars roll toward the end of the assembly line; that's a C5 behind the C6.**

When engineers and designers first started to develop a sixth-generation Corvette, they focused on finding ways for its pieces to come together better during the manufacturing process so that the car's overall quality would be significantly improved.

When fully, assembled, all the complex lines and shapes of the Corvette come together smoothly.

Four months before the car went on sale, members of the automotive press got behind the wheel of both standard and Z51 2005 Corvettes to weigh their impressions of the car.

Seven

The Critics' Verdict

Newly Upgraded Performance Impresses the Top Experts

"I would love to have the new Corvette somewhere in the state of Wyoming on winding mountain passes—fast sweepers— or some places in California, or on a nice stretch of the German autobahn."

—Robert Lutz, vice president of product development and chairman of GM North America

NO MATTER HOW MUCH THE CORVETTE STAFF test drove prototypes of the new Corvette, the car still needed to pass the ultimate test—getting a thumbs up from the boss, General Motors Vice President of Product Development and Chairman of GM North America Robert Lutz. If Lutz liked the car, chief engineer Dave Hill could rest easier when the car was later shown to the automotive press three months before the car went on sale in the fall of 2004.

Lutz first got behind the wheel of a C6 development car in late 2003 at GM's Milford, Michigan, test track. "On the straights and between the curves, I frequently hit triple digits with the new 'Vette. Just about exactly halfway around the Milford ride road where you come out of a right-hander and then can accelerate hard for a couple hundred yards before you take another sweeping 90-degree right-hander—triple digits. I was absolutely excited and thrilled," he recalls.

The security folks at the giant proving ground sometimes ticket employees for exceeding the ride road's

50-mile-per-hour limit, but Lutz escaped points on his corporate license while he was evaluating the new Corvette. He needed to test whether the car was as composed and comfortable at 100 miles per hour as a normal passenger car is at 50, one of the goal's in the new 'Vette's construction. Lutz also wanted to get a feel for the car's new interior and its performance levels.

"Just prior to taking the wheel for the first time in an early C6, I wanted to get another taste of the C5 for comparison purposes, and it sort of brought back in an instant why the Corvette is so successful," Lutz adds. "When I blasted off in the new C6 development vehicle, though, I was astonished at how much it blew the socks off what is one of today's great sports cars. The C6 has so much more precision and is so much more athletic that I was instantly sold. The handling is truly impressive, much more agile—a leaner and meaner beast."

The ride road at the proving ground simulates the worst roads in the country. "The new Corvette absorbs that very well," Lutz says. "The track goes into a series of

During this evaluation, the journalists drove the new Corvettes on racetracks, test tracks, and public roads.

asphalt two-lane right- and left-handers, including very quick sequences of sharp lefts and rights, with a sprinkling of potholes and even a railroad track. This stretch is succeeded by the long straight with undulating bumps that are designed to get the suspension out of phase, and at the end there is a sharp right-hander that goes over some washboard surface to see if the car will skate outward or if it will maintain traction. If I remember well, I was able to skate with it a little bit over the washboard surface at the track."

"The steering is extremely responsive," he adds. "There's no numbness in it at all. It has good center feel, comes off center very nicely. I just thought it was great."

During his test drive, Lutz had the stability system engaged on the development car he drove, to get the same impression driving the car as a customer would. "The really nice thing about the way we program our vehicle stability system is [that] ideally you do not feel the stability control system—you just think you're one of the world's best drivers and sadly the rest of the world

doesn't recognize it," he says. "Our software guys will define a line all the way around the complex inside perimeter of the physical boundaries of the car so that you can go all the way to the limits in any direction before the system takes over. The system still intervenes to save you from yourself, but you really have to take it to the very edge before it kicks in."

Fighter pilot and exotic car collector Lutz also reports that he didn't drive so hard as to activate the anti-lock braking and that he was able to hold a normal conversation with a passenger during his high-speed drive, confirming that the new car is quieter inside. He also notes that discerning drivers appreciate the sounds that the 2005 Corvette does make. "We've deliberately tried to do a relatively gentle exhaust note and not have the 'boy racer' roar. What we wanted is an almost BMW-like, 'executive express' feeling. This is a serious driver's car, not a drag racer."

The Corvette's interior design also caught Lutz's eye. "The first thing I noticed is that this is a very serious driver's car from the way everything is arranged—your

At Virginia International Raceway, the drivers were allowed to put the cars through their paces.

Before these sessions, Robert Lutz, GM's vice president of product development and chairman of GM North America, did his own test drive of the car, which he was very impressed with.

relationship to the instrument panel, the pedals, the side bolsters on the seats, the whole ergonomics area," he says. "The fact that there is a lot of functional black on the inside conveys a very strong impression of a car that was done for people who are serious about driving. In fact, ergonomically, everyone's comment is [about] the enormous amount of room in the car, [how] it feels one whole class larger."

"Overall, it comes across as a great leap forward—as every new generation of Corvette needs to make," he adds. "It looks great, has wonderful interior packaging, is ergonomically pleasing, and has great performance and precision. We have perhaps one of the best interiors we've done so far at General Motors in terms of detailing and little touches and so forth. It's fast, and we've spent a great deal of time making sure it has a very stiff structure

and it just feels, dare I say, a lot more like a European sports car. And, like all the 'Vettes, I think it represents amazing value for what we're going to charge for it."

With such gushing praise, Dave Hill, Corvette chief engineer, felt pretty confident that the car would get similar accolades from the press after it was shown at the Detroit auto show in January 2004. "The response has been great. It goes without saying that we're very happy," he says.

Yet after that first outing, some critics said the 2005 Corvette's styling broke no new ground and that while Maserati, Ferrari, and Lamborghini have all recently made strides in beauty, the Corvette has remained more true to its classic form.

Nonetheless, the crowd clamored to see the new car, and experts from top auto magazines could hardly wait to get behind the wheel. They did that in late May 2004, taking a five-hour tour through the Smokey Mountains and hill country of southern Virginia, followed by laps on nearby Virginia International Raceway, a 3.2-mile road course that was reconstructed in 2000 and has gotten good reviews from racers.

Automobile Magazine's Tim Ferris was first taken by the sight of the 'Vette's new convertible incarnation after getting a glimpse of it at GM's Detroit hangar before boarding the plane to Virginia. "I liked the C6. If I were going to get one, I'd get the Z51 ragtop. Corvettes have always been dark and claustrophobic and closed-in, so I like the ragtop."

Road & Track's Matt DeLorenzo adds, "After seeing it in the auto shows, it looks more dramatic out on the street. Your eyes are really drawn to the glass on the

Fast laps around the track convinced Larry Webster from *Car and Driver* magazine of the C6's handling improvements.

hatch. This thing doesn't have such a big rear end. I can't help but compare it to a 911. It looks more Euro than it has ever looked, but that's not a knock on the car. It's an American front-engine, rear-drive V-8 car with the sound to match. I've always been a big fan of Corvettes, and this car is what a Corvette should look like."

"I loved it," says Larry Webster, top car tester for *Car and Driver* magazine. "I've got to tell you, I'm a huge fan of the C5, so this is preaching to the choir, but I really liked the C6. The first thing I thought when I got in the car was 'finally they ditched that flimsy seat.' I liked the interior a lot better than the C5's. It had the same V-8 burble, fantastic throttle response, yet the shifter was better. Everything worked; it had more features; it was more comfortable. I thought if this costs the same as the old one, they'll sell every one of them."

Webster, six-foot two, also liked that the 2005 Corvette was very roomy, especially in the driver's seat. "Part of the advantage you get . . . is you're never compromising your driving position. The telescoping

Webster also was surprised by the high levels of grip the car had in corners.

Most of the critics praised the driver comfort and the ease at which the car could be driven quickly.

steering wheel is just a huge addition for someone my size," he notes.

DeLorenzo thought the 'Vette's refined interior was one of its best upgrades. "The seats are better; there's more thigh support. The cabin also is more comfortable, even though the car is shorter. The footwells seem to be

ample, so it's a very comfortable car to drive, and drive quickly and easily."

He particularly noticed the car's high-tech displays on the instrument panel: "The head-up display is improved; the lighting is much better." On the interior as a whole, he concurs that interior has more of a European feel. "It's a

soft-touch, satin finish. The standard car looks a little cheap with its black plastic component part radio," but he added that the uplevel navigation radio looks much better.

GM provided a Porsche 911 as well as C5s for the critics to compare to the new C6s. "On the road, I didn't go super fast, but there was one thing you could say that was wrong with the C5—it had a little floatiness. It just made you a little nervous," Webster says. "The C6 had none of that. It hit mid-corner bumps and it just stayed glued on the road."

"I've always preferred a 'Vette over a 911," he adds. "They made the C6 shorter, but they didn't make it narrower, which is in many ways what it needed. On tight country roads in some ways a 911 is more comfortable because it takes up less of the lane. But on the other hand, I like the Corvette better simply because it's more comfortable and it rides a lot better. Another thing is that you don't have to shift—there's so much torque you can just leave the thing in third and it will pull out of anything."

Back roads in rural Virginia provided everyone with the opportunity to test the car in real-world driving conditions.

Coupes and convertibles, standard and Z51—all of these were driven by the automotive experts.

The critics also noticed that the shorter C6 (left) actually has a slightly longer wheelbase than its predecessor.

Its windshield is also higher, but that change came as the result of new safety regulations.

Critics also noted it was easier to see out of the back of the C6 convertible (left).

The gauges were praised for their simplicity and subtle styling.

Car tester Webster, an admitted Corvette fan, felt that the C6 still feels bigger than a same-size Porsche on the road.

Automobile Magazine's Ferris drove both the standard C6 and ones equipped with the F55 magnetic ride (MR) option and the track-oriented Z51 option. "The Z51 has marvelous handling, and I thought the front end was particularly impressive in the way that it's very well mated with the tires and carves a line beautifully," he says. "The MR would make it easier to drive quickly. If you were going to share the car with a spouse, and you were concerned whether he or she was quite as assured with

bad road conditions, then the MR option would make sense. All of the C6s have tons of brakes. The handling is very predictable, and you don't get any nasty surprises that you didn't invent yourself."

Road & Track's DeLorenzo felt the ride was better in the Z51 than the old Z51. "And out of the two—the Z51 and the MR cars—on a back road, the MR system is better," he says. "There is some body roll in the base car and the Z51 car. On some tight back roads, we were scraping the air dam. There's that much wheel travel and body motion.

"The new shifter is really nice, but you have to be precise in your shifting. You have to be patient. The gates are so close you can get hung up. If you take it easy and get used to it, the shorter throws are pleasant."

Webster spent extra time comparing the standard 2005 Corvette with the Z51 car. "I was trying to make a judgment on the Z51's ride. I still can't imagine why you wouldn't buy the Z51," he says. "I like the way that thing feels; it just seems to communicate a little bit better."

Once on the track, he was even more convinced of his favorite. "The Z51 is the car to have. If there's a ride

penalty, it's just about imperceptible," he says. "I think if you put the Z51 tires on an MR car, the handling would be just about equal. I took the old Z06 out and you realize when you drive that thing how much you are just trying to hold on. The wheel is just too far away. In the new car, I doubt I was going any slower in the Z51 than in the old Z06.

"I shut off all the traction control, and the C6 is very easy to drive on the track; you can trail the brakes and the car will rotate for you. The car has a lot of grip; it seems to hang on better. There were a couple of hairpins that I hit, and I thought 'here's where I'm going to slide,' but I didn't. I did get some pad fade in the base cars. The brake pedal gets a little squishy."

Ferris liked the magnetic ride car better on the track than the road. "The MR car is easier to drive on the track, but on public roads it seems slightly trampy and, personally, I preferred the Z51. They're very much like Corvettes—if you were blindfolded, you'd know you were driving a Corvette. I was impressed by the fact the Corvette folks brought along a 911. Considering the difference in money, there's a lot to be said for the fact that most of what you want to do with a sports car you can do with a base Corvette."

DeLorenzo says his overall impression of the car was that "the C5 drives bigger, but the C6 drives a lot tidier. It feels lighter on its feet. Its turn-in is quicker. It's very well balanced. You can tell right away when you're driving the

The long wheelbase and low stance of the C6 seem more exaggerated on everyday roads.

The testers didn't really get a chance to drive the car in tough weather or road conditions and see if it lives up to the promise of handling well in all types of situations.

Even with its new face, onlookers correctly guessed the C6 as a Corvette.

car that the clutch take-up is lighter and the gearshift is shorter. It's just a much more precise feeling. The car body is tight. And there's more structural integrity in both the coupe and the convertible, so it's very quiet."

"It doesn't explode off the line like you'd expect, but it's more balanced, a lot easier to drive, very tractable at low speeds. The steering is also sharper," he notes.

"The 'Vette's always had its own niche. Nothing under $100,000 touches it," adds Webster, who is unabashed in his affection for the car. "You look at how close you are in price to a Mazda RX8 or a Nissan 350Z, and if you stretch, you can get a 'Vette, and it's incalculably better. I scored it 100 on the last Ten Best test we did. I just love the C6s."

Better visibility and lighting also contributed to more driver comfort on the back roads.

The critics also took time to inspect the car's rear hatch, which still has room for luggage even with its hardtop stowed underneath it.

During long test drives, GM evaluators learned to appreciate the size of the convertible's trunk.

Though some of the critics found the C6 to look too tame, they did like its smaller tail.

Overall, the critics felt that the sixth-generation Corvette was a worthy upgrade of this legendary car, which has seen continued success for 52 years.

Specifications

2005 Chevrolet Corvette

Composite body panels, hydroformed steel frame with aluminum and magnesium components
Manufactured at Bowling Green, Kentucky

Engine — Cast aluminum block and heads, 90-degree overhead valve V-8

Displacement

(liters/cubic inches/cc)	6.0/364/5,970
Bore x stroke (in/mm)	4x3.62/101.6x92
Compression ratio	10.9:1
Horsepower/kw @ rpm	400/298@6,000
Torque lb-ft @ rpm	400@4,400
Pounds per horsepower	7.95
Top speed (mph)	186
Redline	6,500 rpm

Fuel economy mpg city/hwy/combined — 18/29/23 manual, 18/26/21.5 automatic

Six-speed Tremec T56 standard/Z51		Four-speed Hydra-Matic 4L65-E (optional)	
First	2.66:1/2.97:1	First (G-speed standard)	3.06:1
Second	1.78:1/2.07:1	Second	1.63:1
Third	1.30:1/1.43:1	Third	1.00:1
Fourth	1.00:1/1.00:1	Fourth	0.70:1
Fifth	0.74:1/0.71:1	Reverse	2.29:1
Sixth	0.50:1/0.57:1	Final drive standard/	
Reverse	2.90:1/3.28:1	optional	2.73:1/3.15:1
Final drive	3.42:1		

Front and rear suspension — Short/long arm cast aluminum, transverse composite leaf spring

Steering ratio — 16.1:1

Turning circle, curb-to-curb (ft/m) — 39/12

Brake rotor diameter x thickness (in/mm) — F: 12.8x1.26/325x32; R: 12.0x1/305x26

Z51 — F: 13.4x1.26 /340x32; R: 13.0x1/330x26

Wheels/tires: — F: 18x8.5; R: 19x10;
Goodyear Eagle F1 GS Extended Mobility *Standard and Magnetic Selective Ride: Directional; Z51: Asymmetric*
F: P245/40ZR-18; R: P285/35ZR-19

Wheelbase (in/mm)	105.7/2,686
Length (in/mm)	174.6/4,435
Width (in/mm)	72.6/1,844
Height (in/mm)	49.1/1,246
Track (in/mm)	F: 62.1/1,577; R: 60.7/1,542
Curb weight (lb/kg)	3,179/1,442

Weight distribution (f/r %)	51/49
Interior volume (cu ft/L)	52.1/1,475
Head room (in/mm)	37.9/952
Leg room (in/mm)	43/1,093
Shoulder room (in/mm)	55.1/1,403
Hip room (in/mm)	53.7/1,363
Cargo volume (cu ft/L) (coupe)	22.4/634
Fuel capacity (gal/L)	18.0/68.1

2004 Dodge Viper

Composite and aluminum body panels, steel tubular backbone frame
Manufactured at Detroit, Michigan

Engine — Cast aluminum block and heads, 90-degree overhead valve V-10

Engine displacement

(liters/cubic inches/cc)	8.3/505/8,277
Bore x stroke (in/mm)	4.03x3.96/102.4x100.6
Compression ratio	9.6:1
Horsepower/kw @ rpm	500/372@5,600
Torque lb-ft @ rpm	525@4,200
Pounds per horsepower	6.71
Top speed (mph)	190
Redline	6,000 rpm
Fuel economy mpg city/hwy	10/20 manual

Six-speed manual	
First	2.66:1
Second	1.78:1
Third	1.30:1
Fourth	1.00:1
Fifth	0.74:1
Sixth	0.50:1
Reverse	2.90:1
Final drive	3.07:1

Front/rear suspension — Double A-arm, coil springs/double A-arm, coil springs

Steering ratio — 16.7:1

Turning circle, curb-to-curb (ft/m) — 40.5/12.3

Brake rotor diameter x thickness (in/mm) — F: 14.0 x 1.26/355x32; R: 14.0x1.26/355x32

Wheels/tires — F: 18x10; R: 19x13;
Michelin ZP — F: P275/35ZR-18; R: P345/30ZR-19

Wheelbase (in/mm)	98.8/2,510
Length (in/mm)	175.6/4,461
Width (in/mm)	84.8/2,154

Height *(in/mm)*	47.6/1,209
Track *(in/mm)*	F: 61.6/1,565
	R: 60.9/1,547
Curb weight *(lb/kg)*	3,357/1,526
Weight distribution *(f/r percent)*	48/52
Head room *(in/mm)*	36.5/927
Leg room *(in/mm)*	42.4/1,077
Shoulder room *(in/mm)*	54.1/1,374
Cargo volume *(cu ft/L)*	8.0/226
Fuel capacity *(gal/L)*	19.0/71.9

2004 Porsche 911 Carrera

Steel unit body
Manufactured at Stuttgart, Germany

Engine	Cast aluminum block and heads, flat-six, DOHC, 4 valves per cylinder
Displacement	
(liters/cubic inches/cc)	3.6/224/3,596
Bore x stroke *(in/mm)*	3.78x3.26/ 96x83
Compression ratio	11.3:1
Horsepower/kw @ rpm	320/235 @6,800
Torque lb-ft @ rpm	273@4,250
Pounds per horsepower	9.59
Top speed *(mph)*	177
Redline	7,300 rpm
Fuel economy mpg city/hwy/combined	18/26/21 manual

Six-speed manual

First	3.40:1
Second	2.20:1
Third	1.52:1
Fourth	1.22:1
Fifth	1.02:1
Sixth	0.84:1
Reverse	3.55:1
Final drive	3.44:1

Front/rear suspension	Strut, coil springs/multi-link, coil springs
Steering ratio	16.9:1
Turning circle, curb-to-curb *(ft/m)*	34.8/10.6
Brake rotor diameter x thickness *(in/mm)*	F: 12.5x1.10/318x28; R: 11.8x0.95/300x24
Wheels/tires	F: 17x7; R: 17x9; F: P205/50ZR-17; R: P255/40ZR-17
Wheelbase *(in/mm)*	92.6/2,352
Length *(in/mm)*	174.5/4,432
Width *(in/mm)*	69.7/1,770
Height *(in/mm)*	51.4/1,306
Track *(in/mm)*	F: 57.7/1,466; R: 58.3/1,481
Curb weight *(lb/kg)*	3,020/1,373
Weight distribution *(f/r percent)*	51/49

Interior volume *(cu ft/L)*	52.1/1,475
Head room *(in/mm)*	38.0/965
Leg room *(in/mm)*	41.6/1,057
Shoulder room *(in/mm)*	51.7/1,313
Cargo volume *(cu ft/L)*	12.0/340
Fuel capacity *(gal/L)*	16.9/63.9

2004 Ferrari 360 Modena

Aluminum body, steel monocoque
Manufactured at Modena, Italy

Engine	Cast aluminum block and heads, 90-degree DOHC V-8, five valves per cylinder
Displacement	
(liters/cubic inches/cc)	3.6/219/3586
Bore x stroke *(in/mm)*	3.35x3.11/85x79
Compression ratio	11.0:1
Horsepower/kw @ rpm	395/294 @ 8,500
Torque lb-ft @ rpm	275 @ 4,750
Pounds per horsepower	7.75
Top speed *(mph)*	180-plus
Redline	9,000 rpm
Fuel economy mpg city/hwy	11/16 *(manual)*

Six-speed automanual

First	3.29:1
Second	2.16:1
Third	1.61:1
Fourth	1.27:1
Fifth	1.03:1
Sixth	0.85:1
Final drive	4.44:1

Front/rear suspension	Double A-arm, coil springs/double A-arm, coil springs
Turning circle, curb-to-curb *(ft/m)*	35.4/10.8
Brake rotor diameter x thickness in/mm	F: 13.0x1.25/330x32; R: 13.0x1.25/330x32
Wheels/tires	F: 18x7.5; R: 18x9.5; F: P215/45ZR-18; R: P275/40ZR-18
Wheelbase *(in/mm)*	102.3/2,598
Length *(in/mm)*	176.3/4,478
Width *(in/mm)*	75.7/1,923
Height *(in/mm)*	46.6/1,184
Track *(in/mm)*	F: 65.7/1,669; R: 63.7/1,618
Curb weight *(lb/kg)*	3,064/1,393
Weight distribution *(f/r percent)*	51/49
Head room *(in/mm)*	36.5/927
Leg room *(in/mm)*	46.5/1,181
Cargo volume *(cu ft/L)*	12.0/340
Fuel capacity *(gal/L)*	25.1/95

Index

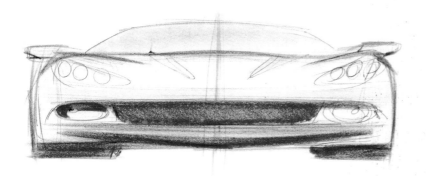
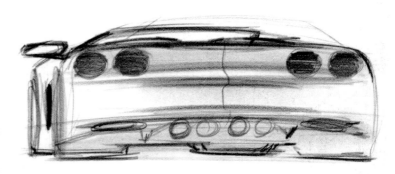
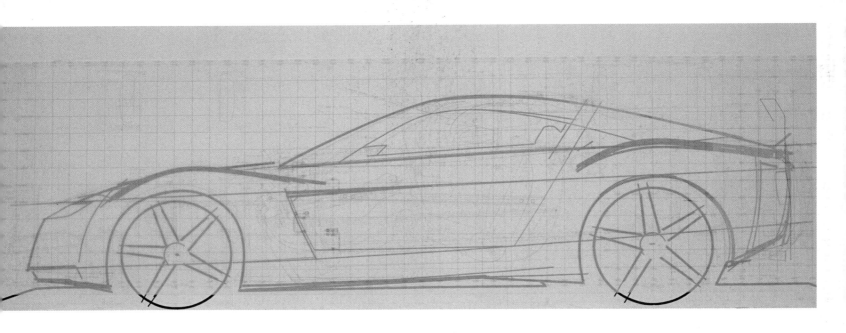
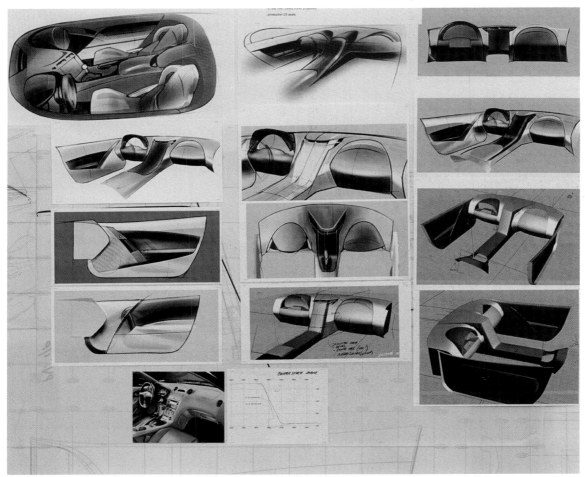